SILENT THINK TIME

How to Bring Virtues Back into Our Home, Schools, Counseling and Work

Karen Zalubowski Stryker

outskirtspress
DENVER, COLORADO

The opinions expressed in this manuscript are solely the opinions of the author and do not represent the opinions or thoughts of the publisher. The author has represented and warranted full ownership and/or legal right to publish all the materials in this book.

Silent Think Time
How to Bring Virtues Back into Our Home, Schools, Counseling and Work
All Rights Reserved.
Copyright © 2012 Karen Zalubowski Stryker
v1.0

Cover Photo © 2012 jupiterimages.com. All rights reserved - used with permission.

This book may not be reproduced, transmitted, or stored in whole or in part by any means, including graphic, electronic, or mechanical without the express written consent of the publisher except in the case of brief quotations embodied in critical articles and reviews.

Outskirts Press, Inc.
http://www.outskirtspress.com

ISBN: 978-1-4327-9331-9

Outskirts Press and the "OP" logo are trademarks belonging to Outskirts Press, Inc.

PRINTED IN THE UNITED STATES OF AMERICA

Dedicated to our five wonderful children and our "emotional firefly" grandchildren, with thanks for my husband's support. And a special thanks for all the inspirations from Paramahansa Yogananda.

Also a special thanks to Carol Sowell of Tucson, Arizona, for giving me ideas on how to expand the book to a greater audience, her terrific insight on how to improve the book's clarity and organization, and her editing to correct all the grammatical or punctuation errors.

Contents

The Concept of Silent Think Time (STT) 1
    STT and Children 3
    STT and Adults 4
    How to Begin STT 5
    My Gift to You 7
Overview 8
Setting Up an STT Room 11
    STT in Schools 11
    STT Should Come First 13
    Set Up Your Own STT Room 13
    Meditation and Grateful Thoughts 16
Universal Acknowledgments 17
    Sixth Sense and Animals 17
    Vocabulary 18
    Our Bodies 18
    Our Planet 21
    About the Yugas 22
    Attitudes and Well-Being 24
    Meditation and Healing 25
    Chakra Chart 29
    Beyond Our Bodies 30
    STT and the Brain 33
Lessons Philosophy 38

Letting Go: Freedom From Beliefs and Ego Release	41
K-12 Students' Early Morning Lessons and Exercises	48
K-12 Students' Focus on "What If?" and "Why?"	52
Suggested What-If Questions for Grade School Students	52
Suggested What-If and Why Questions for Teens, Adults, Counselors, Businesses, Institutions and Organizations	54
Did You or Will You Do This Today?	56
Compassion	56
Self-Discovery	57
Attachment	58
Success	58
Ego-Control	58
Positive Mindset	59
Peace	59
Adults' Silent Think Time Thoughts	62
Adults, Businesses, Institutions & Organizations Healing Exercises	71
Ego and Negative Thought Release Exercises	71
Introspective Thoughts	73
Imagine You Are Gathering Chi/Qi Energies	75
Breathing Exercises	77
Quietly Watch Your Thoughts	78
Self-Vibrate Your Chakras, Create and Review	80
Healthy Hand Hugs and Using True Hugs Liberally	82
What Were the Results of Your Lessons?	84
Appendix A: Some Suggested Sayings to Spark Ideas	86
Compassion	86
Faith	87
Forgiveness	87
Happiness	87
Peace	88
Positive Thinking	88
Self-Discovery	89
Success	90
Anger	91

    Attachment 92
    Change 92
    Ego 92
    Fear 93
    Guilt 93
Appendix B: Some Favorite Poems and Affirmations for Ideas 94
Appendix C: Positive, Affirmative Words for a Happier Life 102
Appendix D: Negative Downfall Words That Destroy
a Happy Life 105
References 109
About the Author 112

The Concept of Silent Think Time (STT)

All teachers, counselors, parents, coaches, business human resource departments, military veterans, prisons, hospitals and nursing homes can benefit from this book. For all of these groups, doing positive "SILENT THINK TIME" (STT) once or twice daily will raise morals, virtues, and brain functioning, and will help everyone who participates to develop the full potential of human consciousness.

Ideally, we should set up STT rooms in all areas of our everyday lives: home, work, school, nursing homes, hospitals, prisons, airports, and bus or train terminals. In STT rooms, everyone in your home, school or these other places can recenter and balance their energies several times daily. You can help change the quality of our educational system, your family and work attitudes by doing your part to have STT rooms and lessons implemented!

Do you want your students, family, clients, employees or inmates to behave in ways that are positively centered, emotionally balanced, peaceful, cheerful, kind, respectful, polite, self-controlled, patient, understanding, wise and peaceful? Have you asked yourself daily, "Who am I in relation to the rest of the world?" and "What was my most precious moment today?" If not, then you can benefit from this book.

The ideas presented here can also improve creativity and academic performance; reduce the effects of attention deficit hyperactivity

◄ SILENT THINK TIME

disorder (ADHD) and other learning disorders; and help people deal with anxiety, depression and substance abuse. Practicing STT can help alleviate post-traumatic stress disorder in children or adults who have experienced any type of violent acts.

By focusing and concentrating during SILENT THINK TIME lessons, your mind will fuel a loving sensitivity that will result in wanting to know others better and creating a happy environment, making ideas flow better throughout the day. These lessons can create a blissful, enlightened mood so one wants to dive deeper into relationships with others. The lessons will stimulate our willpower and reestablish our intuitive selves, keeping us motivated toward the correct pathways in life.

STT is a mindfulness-based stress reduction (MBSR) technique, a form of meditation, which involves focusing one's attention on sensations, feelings and state of mind. This activity has been shown to reduce harmful stress hormones. In one study, researchers took MRI scans of the brains of people who had participated in meditation for eight weeks. The density of the gray matter in the hippocampus increased significantly compared with the control group (see reference 20).

Technology has advanced thousands of times faster than our true understanding of ourselves and our ability to be self-controlled and self-disciplined. Materialistic items have taken precedence over pursuing our true needs for love, balance and becoming centered individuals.

This has created overwhelming greed, violence and imbalance in today's materialistic world. This negative process will only get worse if we do not put in place some measures to balance the thinking of all of us -- from our young children to our elderly.

Because we are chronically sleep-deprived and ill-fed, with unbalanced aura energies, we often make wrong choices in life. If we

THE CONCEPT OF SILENT THINK TIME (STT)

developed a better understanding of ourselves and our true desires, we wouldn't make incorrect choices in vocation, investments, life companions, etc.

We're constantly bombarded by information, creating a sensory overload for those of us living in today's electronic world. To combat the effects of these distracting stimuli, we need to discipline our bodies and minds, like taming the steed. We need to use self-control in order to make righteous, skillful, discreet, correct and bridled decisions.

Sensory stress overload changes our hormones, immune system, brain and entire bodily functions; therefore, we need to slow our stressed activities.

As STT students or as meditators learn to silence the chatter of their minds, reducing the extraneous mental and emotional "noise clutter," we notice they become easier persons to be around because they seem steady, imperturbable and more balanced than others.

STT and Children

Children pay a big price for living in this world of sensory and informational overload. The Internet, videos, iPods, TV and all the rest have turned our young emotionally numb. They create an amplified artificial support crutch, enabling youngsters to hide their pain, rather than communicating to those in their true support system: the families and relatives who love them unconditionally.

We need to teach our children "good cybercitizenship." Good cybercitizenship is the self-disciplined, self-controlled use of positive words and behaviors when interrelating with anyone on the Internet or while texting. Then this loving attitude can spread to our actual daily friend and family relationships.

SILENT THINK TIME

Kids' TV cartoons cause children to be in constant strobe light motion, like "emotional fireflies," thus losing their emotional connections, balance, and knowledge of values, compassion, understanding and concentration. Children under the spell of these frantic, quick-changing video images and loud, wild characters are unable to focus calmly and positively on life's really important matters: family and friends.

By applying STT lessons and positive thinking, we can teach our children to refocus and concentrate on their attitudes and behaviors with serene composure, thereby improving their virtues and morals. If schools would incorporate this philosophy and lessons in all grades, they could help children correct their negative behaviors and find greater peace and maturity.

STT and Adults

Bringing back good virtues and morals aids a person in distinguishing between the principles of right and wrong. It means being in excellent conduct or character and being ethical in thoughts, attitudes and behavior, including sexual activity. It involves having sympathy and respect for others, with a mental mindset of courage, discipline and confidence.

STT is the ability to think deeply by adopting a calm, passive attitude – a neutral mind, in which you do not judge yourself or others. That peaceful, blissful attitude is carried into all your daily activities.

Virtuous people have the effective power or force, efficacy, potency and ability to heal or strengthen themselves or others. They have bravery, uprightness, rectitude, good quality and accomplishment, while being excellent in general valor, courage and daring to do what is just with a sense of duty and responsibility to the world. As in Christian theology the three virtues are faith, hope and charity.

THE CONCEPT OF SILENT THINK TIME (STT)

A thorough application of STT leads to mastering a balanced mind and a clean aura, free from worries, doubts, fears of the future, resentment, anger or shame of the past.

How to Begin STT

STT works by initiating a sequence of physical and mental changes that affect the body, mind, and spirit (our infinite divine soul) simultaneously.

A person can get started with STT by faithfully applying the exercises and lessons described in this book every day. Being aware of all the positive and negative words used in your vocabulary allows you the ability to change. By using your silent imagination, you can change your energy meridians and your chakras, therefore allowing yourself to heal from bad habits, pain and negative energies.

You can ask for your work worlds, schools and counseling arenas to set up an STT room in order to improve creative work production or negative attitudes; correct a student's bad behavior; or help clients solve their own problems.

Many of our workplaces are destroying our morals by allowing a loose tolerance of drugs and alcohol just to keep employees or soldiers happy while doing mundane jobs. Some lessons on self-discipline and self-control during an employer-paid 15-minute SILENT THINK TIME could help correct any negative behaviors.

We seem to be ignorant of the interconnectivity between ourselves and all the other people and living creatures on earth. We as humans are devouring the earth to the point that several hundred species of animals go extinct every year. When we do not see the interconnectivity between all living things, we cannot see the damage being done to our world. We are behaving with an ignorant bias by ignoring this interconnectivity, interdependency and relativity among all humans and the rest of our earth.

We are not being good universal or cosmic citizens if we do not love others as ourselves. This is why it is important on a daily basis to sincerely think, write, discuss and share openly these feelings in positive expressions and awareness of others.

A Tucson, Arizona, school used somewhat similar concepts from the David Lynch Foundation successfully (ref. 2). The school principal found there was a 50 percent decrease in bad behaviors, and students said, "I can sleep better and my thoughts are clearer" and "I don't get frustrated or angry and I stay more relaxed now."

STT goes beyond the David Lynch Foundation in that it applies teaching and focusing techniques in the realities of today's busy world. My book can be easily applied at any level at any place in our society. Review the "Letting Go" chapter and ask yourself, "What if?" and "What can I do to improve my world?" and "Am I using words from the positive or negative lists of words in the appendices?"

Would you like to see the following changes occur?

a. Your students sincerely, compassionately, enthusiastically motivated to shun negative offensive behaviors such as bullying, misunderstanding and being outright mean?

b. Your grade school children being motivated to inspire adults with incredible creativity in their science projects, poems or songs, rather than being defiant, intolerant and incompetent?

c. Yourself with an attitude that promotes the most brilliant ideas at work so that you are promoted in a short period of time, rather than just waiting for the paycheck to come in?

d. Teenagers choosing to be ambitious in helping the handicapped

THE CONCEPT OF SILENT THINK TIME (STT)

    neighbor by carrying their groceries or mowing their lawns rather than robbing them for money for drugs?

e. Your counseling clients to break their drug habits or other bad behaviors rather than having a negative, defeated attitude?

f. Your employees positively and creatively motivated, trustworthy, respectful, accomplished and grateful, rather than calling in sick often and doing the minimum amount of work?

g. All your friends and relatives to be righteous, ethical, faithful, honest, presumptive, virtuous and well conducted with integrity rather than backstabbing you at their first opportunity?

h. Your pains healed and yourself rid of bad habits forever rather than dwelling in self-centered pity?

My Gift to You

After gathering five college degrees – in psychology, computer science, art and two in education -- and seven teaching endorsements, I taught K-12, mostly at the high school level. I used some of these lessons during that time. I found that STT techniques helped my students to focus, concentrate and behave with a positive attitude toward others.

This book was originally started so our 5 children could absorb this information on their own time. In trying to improve their worlds I discovered how much more I could learn in this process. Being a person always needing to bring balance to my world by frequently being in a quiet natural environment, focusing on ideas and projects, or just being in a silent meditation mode, I thought others could benefit from my secret of success and STT information.

Overview

This book can benefit readers by helping to rebuild their positive, creative, inborn mindsets. Our intuitive sixth sense can be awakened through positive SILENT THINK TIME.

By setting aside 15 to 50 minutes a day, preferably at the beginning of the day and again later in the day, we can gradually reset ourselves and our society in a more constructive, positive manner. We should *never* fail to see the extreme importance of this for our future! STT is effective whenever we need to be recentered again, such as mid-morning and mid-afternoon.

Incorporating this philosophy can eliminate millions of dollars spent yearly on psychological problems and programs in our society. This reflects not only in our schools, homes, workplaces and counseling practices, but also in society's security forces, hospitals and other institutions, and in everyone's ability to be happily productive in their worlds.

Children are like seeds. If you plant a seed in the ground, you must not take it out to see if it is germinating. You must tend to it carefully daily in order to see the plant grow up and be productive. Therefore we must plant these positive seeds in our children's minds: their ability to be self-controlling and self-disciplined. We have ignored for too long the importance of planting the right seeds in our children's minds.

OVERVIEW

In today's society of constant TV, tweets, texts and Internet drama, we are getting numb to our true basic needs of life: love and happiness. We regard a person as having authority simply on the basis of their fame, position, power, good looks and wealth, rather than on what we find emotionally convincing and reliable. As smart as our brains are, we are easily bought off by superficiality, renouncing our true feelings, emotions and intuitiveness. How shallow we are becoming so quickly.

We are reaching a point in our world where negative actions have the potential to increase, while positive actions are being destroyed. We are channeled to becoming better, smarter and faster than the next person in order to succeed. This inflates our ego, therefore unbalancing our center selves.

But in order to truly succeed, we must keep our behaviors in positive balance. By self-control, humbleness, wisdom and self-discipline, we can keep our egos in balance.

Years ago I remember crying over tender, emotional, dramatic TV movies. People today have turned numb to having sympathy about others' suffering. It shows especially in many of the "blood-splattering" children's and adult video games and action movies. Extreme violence is played out constantly in the news and entertainment media, dwelling on negativity rather than the positive. This mindset could be altered if society would only make the efforts to change it.

Why does our society create so many hurtful, deadly, sensational, action cop movies and videos? We need more images that show our children how to be more introspective and better, more positive-behaving humans on our earth, through helpful, productive actions.

Notice how many words from the TV, Internet and video games are found in the list of "Negative Downfall Words That Destroy a

◀ **SILENT THINK TIME**

Happy Life" in Appendix D. What happened to our genuine love and compassion and the various positive feelings listed in Appendix C, "Positive Affirmative Words?"

The remedy is acknowledging this extremely important downfall of humanity and trying to repair it immediately before more societal damage is done.

Being in a throwaway, wasteful, "drama-devouring" society, can we ever be knowledgeable enough to change our culture?

Will we deceive ourselves or misrepresent ourselves in order to achieve our selfish ends? Can we expand our emotions outwardly and change our broken system through more sympathetic, compassionate, loving ways?

Setting Up an STT Room

Why can't we have SILENT THINK TIME (STT) rooms in all our homes, schools, businesses, hospitals, airports, prisons, etc., just so we can do our STT and meditation?

STT in Schools

"Silent Time in Our Arizona Education System Is Required By Law!" I was told by two retired Douglas, Arizona, teachers that it is written into the Arizona state's educational system laws that the 15 minutes per day is allowed for "silent time." It can be used for saying the Pledge of Allegiance or honoring people who have died. We could be using this "silent time" as "think time" in order to help children develop respect, consideration, understanding, patience and unconditional love, resulting in a rise in our morality and virtues in our schools, counseling and our homes. These results can happen if these lesson concepts are followed daily.

In my travels around the world, I noticed that something like SILENT THINK TIME was being used in schools in many countries. Every day at mid-morning, children were asked to put their heads down on their desks for several minutes while the room remained quiet. Or there would be an afternoon break when children would lie on mats to calm themselves and slow down. Seeing this made me aware of what our

SILENT THINK TIME

American school systems are missing—time when children can stop jumping from one activity to another and get in touch with calmer emotions and their own thoughts. It occurred to me that this constant frantic activity must be why my "emotional firefly" grandchildren cannot settle down long enough to focus on reading books I give them.

When I was young, we paid respect to others and our country by saying the "Pledge of Allegiance" or mentioning our war heroes in the early morning at school. We also had to put our heads down when we got too noisy or the entire class got "time out," and we had rugs to lie on.

This SILENT THINK TIME is no longer used in schools, but it is needed to calm the nervous system. Once the nervous system is calmed down, children can focus on their inner positive selves again, therefore changing any negative behaviors and thus being more successful. These old techniques did work and could be modified for today's world!

One reason we have rebellious children is because they are not getting this quiet time and opportunity to focus on finding their identities. The teachers and parents both push to maximize the time schedule to teach more topics and take more tests, thus pushing students to work faster. The student tries to keep up, as this competition is the key to their getting love and attention from everyone around them. This also creates a stress of not being appreciated for who they truly are.

Rather than spending millions yearly on solving problems created by drugs, violence, social unrest and destruction, why can't we put some time and money into our schools, homes, work and counseling programs to prevent such abnormal behaviors before they develop? Anything that contradicts experience and logic should be abandoned. History can repeat itself in very negative ways if we deny what we have learned. Making introspective time daily for children's moral improvement can prevent negative behaviors that harm everyone around them and damage young people mentally and physically.

SETTING UP AN STT ROOM

STT Should Come First

Unless a specific time is committed to this SILENT THINK TIME, there will always be other obligations. It is important to give yourself the love, respect, kindness and especially the quality of time to yourself to focus and concentrate while silently doing nothing but meditating or reading, reviewing and writing these exercises. It is important that we provide the same quality time to our children as their minds are developing.

We must be reintroduced to the reverence of human courage and nature of life and begin balancing the values of human emotions and affection.

We could avoid violence in our schools, media, homes and workplaces, therefore creating fewer negative downfalls that destroy happiness by cold indifference. Negative behaviors could be offset by sending children to a SILENT THINK TIME in a quiet, sunny room each day, keeping them occupied by positive thinking lessons, as in this book.

San Francisco officials opened North America's first airport yoga room on January 2, 2012, after a passenger suggested it. The 150-square-foot (14 square meters) studio room, just past security in Terminal 2, was converted from a storage room and is free from all noise and cell phones. Yoga mats are provided.

Set Up Your Own STT Room

You could ask for a similar quiet room to be set up at your business, school, home, organization or institution, in order to create your own STT space. Please do yourself and the world around you a favor by pushing for an STT room wherever one can easily be created -- for example: an unused closet, storage room, bedroom, classroom, space in your garage or workshop, or on a roof that has plants or peaceful natural outdoor setting.

SILENT THINK TIME

Ask your spouse at home, boss at work, school principal, school counselors, coaches, hospital administrator, assisted living or nursing home director, or prison chief if they want you to be more productive or calmer. It would be worthwhile for them to create an STT room or time-out area, where individuals could go for about 15 minutes to balance and recenter their bodies, while focusing on these lessons. Tell the administrators that you will guarantee they will see results. Maybe you could even offer to help up set the STT room.

To set up your STT room or area all you need is the following: a serene, noninterrupted, quiet location with natural light; some yoga mats or simple stools (preferably facing eastward for better energy flow); happy plant or animal landscape posters; and a couple of vases of flowers or live plants. Add a long, thin altar-like table facing east for photos of your loved ones or divine spirit, electric imitation candles (avoid potential fire hazards) and several copies my book for people to share when they use the room.

Please remember to put a sign on the STT room door, setting out some important conditions. For example, "Before entering the room please shut off all cell phones. Absolutely no talking or distractions to others. No eating, drinking or smoking allowed. Maximum usage: three hours."

By putting a minimal amount of time aside each day, we could make some immense changes in the lives of ourselves and future generations! Please consider these positive, simple, mind-altering virtuous lessons to help all of us take healthy steps into our future.

Ask your principal, boss or parents to make the daily early morning announcements over the intercom: "It's SILENT THINK TIME." Consider helping install these STT rooms in all of your everyday worlds, institutions, travel stops and airports near you.

SETTING UP AN STT ROOM

You can set up non-secular STT areas by placing your favorite photos of your beloved family members, pets and neighbors on a table. If the school or business doesn't have a separate room available for STT, you could suggest a corner of a room, or ask to use part of the cafeteria or conference room at certain times of the day. A screened wooden or cloth panel helps to block space from others' interruptions.

It is most preferred to find a silent spot with a closed door and thicker walls. Don't be afraid to ask: Remember "Nothing ventured, nothing gained."

For example, my STT and meditation room is a screened off 5-by-8-foot area in my bedroom. It has a small table cabinet with standing and walled pictures of Jesus Christ (ref 34), Mother Theresa, Krishna, Paramahansa Yogananda, other saints, gurus and sages, along with photos of loved ones and one of me in a meditative posture. Also available are my favorite prayers, affirmations and physical exercises. Next to it is a bookcase of my special introspective books, DVDs and CDs.

In front of the photos are two candles, my unopened yet still fragrant Nag Champa incense, and a bag of dried rose petals from the roses in our yard. The flowers were dedicated in honor of all the avatars, saints, gurus and sages who have helped others on this earth. Fresh flowers are preferred but usually donated on special occasions, like birthdays or deaths of our loved ones. Also a little armless stool with a wool blanket on top, facing east, is used for the grateful beginning and after the physical exercise is done.

Another suggestion is to build a glass room or a bottle building like I did for another meditation area at our home. I had 1500 bottles donated to me from local restaurants in 1 ½ months; with a little bribing from my homemade chocolate coconut M&M cookies. The labels must be soaked and removed before mudding them into the wall to close off the porch. It is my way also to show we can save our earth dumps and enjoy the cathedral effect with the beautiful play of light off the multicolored bottles and shapes. Another plus of building a bottle building is that it's cheap to build. Note back of the book "About the Author" for photos.

Meditation and Grateful Thoughts

The difference between STT and mediation is that STT, like a prayer, will allow you to be humble, be honest and ask questions to your imaginary friend, family member, relative or inner omnipresent spiritual soul energy, while expressing complete gratitude for their helping to give you insight into the problems in your life. In deep meditation you feel a sweet comfort of peace, a subtle joy of fulfillment and completeness, and an upwelling thrill of love that accompanies devotional thoughts of God. In that state you have touched the consciousness of the soul – the reflection of the Infinite godly soul within you – and at least momentarily you experience the true joy of freedom from bondage to the mortal body and ego.

As with all the Great Ones' achievements, similarly our challenge is to maintain our connection with that meditation-resurrected consciousness and its gifts of divine grace, and cede to it the reign over our life, attitudes and reactions. With the humble cooperation with the Universal Good, without self-proclamation, you can help yourself and others dispel darkness from the world.

Have you held hands with your family members daily at the table before eating and before bedtime, telling them how you truly love them? Did you tell them you are so grateful they are in your world? Did you ask them what their most precious moment was today? When doing these lessons, it will help you be more aware how this is lacking in your world.

Universal Acknowledgments

This chapter lists many factual statements that are understood throughout the world. These scientific acknowledgements state the extreme importance of the interconnectivity between our attitudes and the well-being of our bodies. They also show how vibrational frequencies affect our chakra Chi/Qi energy flows through our spine, brain and outer auric fields; how yoga and meditation can unclog our energy flows by activating the glands in our bodies, therefore healing us.

By keeping a correct mind, body and soul balance, we can alert our mind's sixth sense and intuition, thus allowing us to heal ourselves and have the ability to embrace ourselves for who we are.

Sixth Sense and Animals

1. Animals have a sixth sense and intuition better than ours. As humans get older, we lose that ability to sense things that are not perceived by our five senses of sight, hearing, taste, smell and touch. Children's simplistic, realistic, intuitive sixth sense abilities are better than those of adults. We need to wake up and improve our faded, sleeping, positive, creative, intuitive sixth sense.

2. How do birds know when to fly south? How do whales and porpoises know when to migrate in the oceans? How do salmon know when to go hundreds of miles to the ocean only to return to their

SILENT THINK TIME

rivers to spawn before they die? Restless horses and snakes are used in China to predict earthquakes. Bees will eventually replace drug-sniffing dogs (ref. 1). How do ants perform their function and remain loyal and cooperative in their massive numbers?

3. Why is it that we often are better able to show our true feelings to our dogs and cats than to our own family members, friends, neighbors and work acquaintances? This is not healthy for human and harmonic connectivity throughout our earth.

4. Dinosaurs lived hundreds of millions of years on earth but we humans have only been here a few thousand years. As smart as our brains are at producing technology, we will self-destruct by not having a balance among our intellects, our emotions and our intuitive sixth sense.

5. Worldwide, some people use self-controlled willpower to predict events, and discover extra powers by focusing their energies to gather information. Are these premonitions like a sixth sense intuition? Can we develop this willpower in a positive manner to help our society by changing our own thinking?

Vocabulary

6. We are still in the "fight or flight" mode of responding to events with negative thinking as our weapons. We need to develop or adopt a positive way of thinking before our "fight or flight" instinct takes over.

7. Have you noticed how there are more positive words in our vocabulary than negative words? See Appendix C, "Positive Affirmative Words," and Appendix D, "Negative Downfall Words." Why is it we use more negative words daily than positive words?

Our Bodies

8. Eating mostly lightly cooked fresh vegetables and fresh fruits, with little meat and carbohydrates or sugars, and avoiding

UNIVERSAL ACKNOWLEDGMENTS

stimulants like caffeine, nicotine or alcohol, will calm the body's nervous system and our energy chakra fields, thus allowing us the ability to relax easily. Chakras are "force centers" or whorls of energy permeating from seven points on the physical body. They are considered focal points for the reception and transmission of energies. Greasy, salty, acidic foods upset our energy balance soon after consumption and have negative effects on our energy auric fields. Vitamins can help repair your body some too (ref. 3-4). Try to cook daily with red onions, garlic and chopped fresh ginger to eliminate most viruses and allergies.

9. Also, by not eating after 6 p.m. in the evening we can get the sleep that is so important for the next day's energy and relaxation. If we were not so ill fed and chronically sleep-deprived, we would be recalling our important dreams, which give us insight, into whom we are. Dreams are displayed on our brain's subconscious movie screen and can send us important messages if we carefully listen to and watch them. This is done during the 3:00 AM until 6:00 AM time frame. Then it is important to wake up early with the sunrise to resynchronize our body energy fields, and not stay up late, in order to ensure a healthier body, mind and soul.

10. Daily physical exercise is important just as is nurturing the "body electric," also known as the aura, through outdoor activities, meditation, yoga, dance, listening to good music, resolving mental conflicts, grounding yourself by connecting with the earth, massage or acupuncture. All of these exercises help us discharge high levels of electrosmog, the invisible electromagnetic radiation resulting from the use of wireless technology and electricity. Electrosmog is thought to be responsible for a condition known as electrosensitivity (ES) or electrohypersensitivity (EHS), which can cause headaches, disruptive sleep patterns, chronic fatigue and other symptoms.

SILENT THINK TIME

Another area of modern life that can be affected by STT is the human biofield, or layers of the human aura. These layers include:
- the physical body
- the energy body, which is the realm of our autonomic nervous system and energy meridians
- the mental body that extends into infinity and contains a record of all life events, thoughts, beliefs and attitudes
- the intuitive body, which is the collective unconscious
- the spiritual body, which is our knowing, awareness, self-healing and our connection with the Divine (ref. 26)

11. According to a Gallup Poll, in 2002, 58 percent of Americans had sleep disorders or insomnia, and that number has risen to almost 82 percent in 2011. Our chemically electronic bodily brain atoms have great difficulty in getting rebalanced; sleep is necessary to help recenter our minds. The only way to correct this is through daily STT practices.

    By letting our conscious mind sleep soundly, we can then soothe our subconscious mind, which remains restless 24-7. Without enough sleep, we cannot truly enter the STT meditative thought pattern of asking the questions listed in this book or being creative with the exercises described in the "Did You or Will You" chapter. Be sure you get enough sleep, and then proceed to the STT lessons.

12. Headaches are typical among people who have allergies to gluten, coffee, wheat, cheese, wine, pickles, mushrooms, sugar and salt hidden in many of our foods.

    Also, it is important to drink one liter of non-boiled natural water daily in order to cleanse the body of toxins, to balance our electrolytes, and rid us of headaches. One cup of non-boiled water before bedtime also can help prevent strokes and heart attacks.

UNIVERSAL ACKNOWLEDGMENTS

Our Planet

13. We know that the earth's magnetic field is related to the earth's rotating molten core. The thought sphere of the human mind is located in the earth's magnetic field, which has been weakened dramatically over the last ten years.

    In physics there is a parameter called Schumann's resonance, which refers to the earth's vibrational frequency. For more than a century, this frequency was measured as 7.80 cycles per second. Since 1987, the frequency has been rising and is now 11 cycles per second and is continuing to increase dramatically. By the end of 2012 it is likely to be 13 cycles per second. At that rate the earth's core would stop rotating, and with the magnetic field gone, your mind's past experiences could vanish. Currently, we have a lot of energy "noise clutter" influencing vibrational frequencies, which is upsetting our weather patterns (ref. 27).

    The study of fossil records shows this happens every 11,000 years, when man will enter into a new state of altered consciousness when the increase in the earth's resonance occurs. This change will determine how our body's electrons think and behave in the future. The Bible, Mayan, Indian and other religious documents mention this turning point, and how important it is for 144,000 human energies to think positive in order to convert this earth's imbalance. Unconditional love and positive thinking are very crucial during this unusual quantum physical era.

    From December 21-23, 2012, our sun will be crossing the middle band or galactic equator of the Milky Way, and earth will be located in the "dark rift," which contains the magnetic axis of the supermassive, spinning black hole located in the center of our galaxy. Our planet will be literally sailing the "cosmic sea" for three days as it did in ancient times (ref. 28).

◄ SILENT THINK TIME

About the Yugas

14. The cycle of the Yugas gives us insight into the past, present, and future development of mankind, changing the consciousness of mankind, his development and civilizations. The yugas describe a cycle of human development that not only predicts highly advanced ages in the future, but indicates that they have occurred in the past too. We learned there are ages of ignorance and darkness, and ages so much more advanced than our own present age that we cannot fully comprehend them.

The yugas tradition in India goes back thousands of years. Sri Yukteswar's year of 1894 book, *The Holy Science,* had many predictions come true, including the twentieth century discovery that energy underlies all matter, and Einstein's $E=mc^2$, all was based on the changing yugas. He dissected the Christian and Dharma scriptures with the scalpel of intuitive reasoning, separating interpolations and wrong interpretations from scholars, while seeking to establish fundamental truths of creation and to describe the evolution and involution of the world. (ref 32)

His book describes a recurring cycle of human development, called the cycle of the yugas, or ages. The complete cycle is made up of an ascending half, or arc and a descending half, or arc, each lasting 12,000 years. In the ascending arc of 12,000 years, mankind evolves through four distinct ages, reaches the peak of development, and then devolves through the four ages in reverse order, in another 12,000 years of the descending arc. Thus in the course of 24,000 years, mankind rises in knowledge and awareness, and again falls, in a cycle that occurs again and again. (ref 33)

We learned from Oriental astronomy that moons revolve around their planets, and planets turning on their axes revolve with their moons round the sun, with its planets and their moons, takes some star to revolve round it in about 24,000 years of our

UNIVERSAL ACKNOWLEDGMENTS

earth – a celestial phenomenon which causes the backward movement of the equinoctial points of the zodiac. (ref 32)

Based on Sri Yukteswar's book, teacher of Paramahansa Yogananda (author of *Autobiography of a Yogi*), we have recently passed through the low ebb in that cycle (Kali) and are moving forward to a higher age – an Energy Age (Dwapara) that will revolutionize the world. They declared that we would live in a time of great social and spiritual change, and much of what we believe would be transformed and uplifted.

Sri Yukteswar says we are currently ascending half of the cycle, in the second stage, called Dwapara. As we advance in this cycle mankind will communicate telepathically; will understand the laws of thought that underlie energy; will overcome the limitations of time; and will perceive Divine consciousness as underlying all reality. He explains that these consciousness changing cycles are caused from influences outside our solar system and effect our perception, awareness, and intellect.

We know that the tiniest atom is capable of being transmuted into vast amounts of energy, objects in space do not move in straight lines because space itself is curved and the universe is finite. The speed of light is the only constant in the universe – all else is measurable only in relation to that constant. Physicists now conceive of the atom as a tiny area of space in which objects fad in and out of the quantum sub-atomic world. String theory goes further saying quarks are made up of even smaller vibrating strings and rings of energy. (ref 33)

In growing up, we understood our world to be made of matter, interacted with energy, but now we learned our world to be made up of energy, assuming the form of matter. (ref 33)

The current theory of the development of mankind is linear, but many facts do not fit into this logic, such as DNA mapping and radiometric dating. We still cannot understand why or how the

◄ SILENT THINK TIME

2500 BC to 2900 BC Pyramids of Giza or the 7000 year old Sphinx or the Incas built their pyramids with extreme accuracy. How did they place 2.5 million 70 ton blocks at an average rate of one block every four minutes for twenty years, when we do not have the intelligence nor tools to do it today? They only had wood, stone, or copper tools, and plaited ropes then. Some of the 3000 BC ancient ruins near the Pakistan's Indus River shows more sophisticated ruins than the more recent ruins. (ref 33)

Other examples, are the very old Nazca plains in Peru, which have huge drawings of animals in such a large scale that they would have to be recognizable only by air; or the 2000 year old Greek Antikythera device that contained over 120 highly precise clockwork gears – evidence of higher knowledge in the past. (ref 33)

The yuga cycles are described by Swami Shanmuga & Amma Adi Sakthi as follows: (1) Kali (winter) and is called the Material Ages; (2) Dwapara (autumn) is called the Energy Age; (3) Treta (spring) is called the Mental Age; and (4) Satya (summer) is called the Spiritual or Golden Age. Height, age, pleasures, sorrows, wants, virtues and sins transcend into mankind in various degrees during these cycles; with kali being the least desired and Satya being the most desired. People's age, height, pleasures, and virtues, will almost double with each cycle, while sorrows, wants and sins will decrease substantially with each cycle for the next yuga cycle.

Mankind has just emerged from the darkest Kali cycle into our present Dwapara cycle in 1900 AD, which is the beginning of the expansion of knowledge, awareness and perception.

Attitudes and Well-Being

15. Almost everyone has been brought up with life-negative attitudes and conditioning against the body. Well-meaning attempts by parents and teachers to "civilize" children and help them to be accepted into society often end up repressing their natural

exuberance, vitality, the sharpness of their senses and the curiosity about their own bodies. When we are aware of the hidden elements of that upbringing, these unconscious attitudes lose their power over us and we can make new life-affirmative choices (ref. 16). This is why it is so important to teach only with positive language while trying to eliminate the negative behaviors and language. Attitudes are the forerunners of conditions.

16. Our careers reward and force us to be critical perfectionists, in order to do exceptionally well at work. It causes us to judge the rest of the world as being less valuable than ourselves, making us more arrogant and creating disrespectful prima donnas blind to their own flaws.

Meditation and Healing

17. STT or meditation can help bring about well-being; spiritual healing – a sense of deep connection to life, compassion and peace of mind; and physical healing. Hundreds of studies indicate that meditation creates a unique hypometabolic state, in which the metabolism is in an even deeper state of rest than during sleep. The studies revealed the following:

    a. Meditation is the only activity that reduces blood lactate, a marker of stress and anxiety.

    b. The calming hormones melatonin and serotonin are increased and the stress hormone cortisol is decreased.

    c. STT has a profound effect upon three key indicators of aging: hearing ability, blood pressure and vision of close objects.

    d. Long-term meditators experience 80 percent less heart disease and 50 percent less cancer than non-meditators.

    e. People who meditate secrete more of the youth-related hormone DHEA than non-meditators. This helps decrease stress, heighten memory, preserve sexual functioning and control weight.

◄ SILENT THINK TIME

    f. Some 75 percent of insomniacs were able to sleep normally when they meditated.

    g. About 34 percent of people with chronic pain significantly reduced their medication when they began meditating (ref. 17).

18. We have learned that Reiki healing, which is similar to STT positive thinking, can detoxify, cleanse and harmonize the body in a holistic and biological healing process. By focusing on the ailing body part we can heal it through vibratory thought patterns transmitted to our brains, like radio waves. The affected part of the body can receive these radiolike waves in order to heal any ailments (ref. 15). The meaning of the following symptoms can help us understand our ailments.

    a. A heart attack is a great accumulation of aggressive energy that has not been lived out.

    b. Arteriosclerosis indicates resistance, tension, rigidity and narrow-mindedness.

    c. High blood pressure indicates unexpressed thoughts and emotions that have not been "let go."

    d. Heartburn is an unconscious attempt to vent your anger.

    e. Constipation has to do with greediness and wanting to hold onto materialistic things.

    f. Hemorrhoids are a problem of letting go of fears.

    g. Gallstones are from bitterness and aggression, turned to stone, thus not letting go of the past.

    h. Impotency from prostate gland problems is due to false judgments, opinions, pessimistic attitude, blaming others, while an unconscious feeling of guilt plays a role in it.

UNIVERSAL ACKNOWLEDGMENTS

 i. Skin problems are associated with overly sensitive people.

 j. Rashes are an insecurity that has caused suppressed emotions that are forcibly making themselves felt (ref. 15).

Some medical systems teach that certain body parts correspond to certain emotional states. When the trauma or negative emotion related to the disease is released, the energy flow is restored and the health issue resolves itself. It is very important to avoid letting some physical or emotional substances or situations into our energy fields because they will lower our vibrational frequencies.

All electron matter generates electrical and electromagnetic energy fields, same as our auras, at a precise frequency, which affect everyone and everything. People with disease and negative emotional states have lower frequencies, for example, a frequency of 100-250. On the other hand, people with higher vibration or harmonic resonance have the energy of unconditional love or the divine energy; their frequencies are 350-400 (ref. 26).

So eat a lot of vegetables and fruit, get solid uninterrupted sleep, and hug often, to keep your body healthy through high-vibrating auric fields meanwhile spreading that good energy to everyone around you. Research has shown that people live longer regardless of their religious affiliation when they practice high harmonic resonance through healthy self-healing methods such as the STT described in this book (ref. 26).

19. Our lymphatic system has no pump until a person moves it. If it is not moving then disease, toxins and stress accumulate; this affects the colors of our body energy auras and our acupuncture bodily energy-flowing hot spots. By unclogging these meridians through a meditative STT, physical movement, acupuncture

(ref. 22), reflexology (ref. 14) or Reiki healing, a person can stay healthy and be more productive in our everyday world (ref. 12).

20. The imbalance in the pineal gland area, the area between the two hemispheres, near our crown (which controls the nucleus projection of everybody's cells) can be balanced through STT and meditation. Bad habits can be broken if one focuses on balancing this area.

21. It is the pulsation of the third eye that regulates the pituitary gland (which is next to the hypothalamus, across from the pineal gland near the forehead) and our lymphatic meridians; that activates the intuition. This imbalance is what results in unhealthy habits or addictions. Focusing on turning the pineal gland into a balanced rhythm, by imagining the shutting off of your bad habit, can make your bad habit disappear. Another method is to temporarily press on your temples to have the same effect.

22. We know that the thymus gland (located behind the upper breastbone side central area) is the most important gland in the maintenance of our immunological system (ref. 15). Knock lightly against it with your fingertips 10 to 20 times to stabilize your system. It has also been an important factor in prevention and treatment of cancer and many other ailments associated with the meridians (ref. 12).

23. Each of our chakras has a gland associated with it. It is why we can mediate on a particular chakra and have it respond with a great amount of energy, healing the areas around it. Be aware of the glands associated with each of the chakras as you read the following summary of the chakras:

UNIVERSAL ACKNOWLEDGMENTS

Chakra Chart

Chakra	Color	Physical Area	Glands	Musical Note/ Strengths/Addictions
ROOT	Red	Spinal Base Reproductive	Adrenal	Security, Survival, Sex, Alcohol, Exercise, C
SPLEEN	Orange	Uterus, Kidney	Gonads	Intimacy, Attachment, Sugar, Alcohol, Emotional Feelings, D
SOLAR PLEXUS	Yellow	Liver	Pancreas	Will, Beliefs, Perfection, Food, Caffeine, Rational, Analytical Thinking, E
HEART	Green	Lungs, Lymph	Thymus	Giving, Receiving, Forgiving, Trust, Love, Harmony, Codependency Balance, F,
THROAT	Blue	Neck, Nose, Ears	Thyroid	Communications, Breath, Healing, Self-Expression Creativity, G,
3RD EYE	Indigo	Auto Nervous System	Pituitary	Intuition, Surpass Service to Others Addiction, A,
CROWN	Violet	Top of Head Central Nervous System	Pineal	Compassion, Non Attachment, Nonreactive, B

◄ SILENT THINK TIME

Beyond Our Bodies

23. The effects of STT have many similarities with the results of yoga. The following ancient forms of yoga have been taught and practiced for thousands of years and are now taught and practiced all over the world:

    a. Hatha yoga (physical exercises/asanas)

    b. Mantra yoga (working with sacred Sanskrit sound and vibration)

    c. Kundalini yoga (working directly with the chakras through spinal energy exercise)

    d. Kriya yoga (working with the breath/pranayama)

    e. Japa yoga (chanting out loud to reprogram the unconscious)

    f. Bhakti yoga (devotion/surrender)

    g. Karma yoga (service and action)

    h. Nada yoga (working with outer and inner sounds)

    i. Dhyana yoga (various ancient meditation techniques, such as working with visualization and mantras)

    j. Jnana yoga (receiving and contemplating the teachings realization of the day).

24. Ancient tonal hymns for DNA repair used certain frequencies for spiritual awakening and transformation of the chakras. These original sound frequencies were apparently used in ancient chants, such as the hymn to St. John the Baptist, which had the power to penetrate into the subconscious mind.

    Our modern-day musical scale (the note A equals 440 Hertz [Hz]) is slightly out of sync with the original solfeggio frequencies. Note the six original solfeggio frequencies below:

    UT – 396 Hz – Liberating Guilt & Fear

UNIVERSAL ACKNOWLEDGMENTS

   RE – 417 Hz – Undoing Situations & Facilitating Change
   MI – 528 Hz – Transformation/Miracles (DNA Repair)
   FA – 639 Hz – Connecting/Relationships
   SOL – 741 Hz – Awakening Intuition
   LA – 852 Hz – Returning to Spiritual Order

Notice how each of the six solfeggio frequencies corresponds not only to a note on the tonal scale, but to a cycle per second Hz frequency number, to a specific color, and ultimately to a particular chakra in the body (ref. 19). This is additional proof of why it is so important to keep ourselves centered and balanced, after being saturated in white noise and electrical junk during our day.

A sound healing therapy meditation using crystal bowls tuned to the these frequencies of 396 Hz and 528 Hz focuses on clearing fear from the body, which starts at the kidneys, the organ related to fear and then moves through the whole body using your voice, breathing and visualization. It also is good for grounding and tuning your body's energy field to the earth's natural vibration. This Sonic Research International sound healing therapy meditation, if practiced for 30 days, is good for activating, and repairing DNA, while healing past injuries or illnesses by awakening your heart to your spiritual divine creator.

25. All persons, regardless of their belief systems, can enrich themselves by realizing the Truth through Kriya yoga, while using some of the Kundalini yoga spinal exercises (ref. 6-7).

Kriya yoga is a positive, scientific path for realization of Truth, free from the burden of philosophizing, ratiocination, fanaticism or sectarian ceremony. It is an eternal direct method of communing with our inner infinite Self, our Lord.

Practicing Kriya initiates a sequence of physical and mental changes that affect the body, mind and soul simultaneously. It is a great way to rebalance our bodies (ref. 8).

◂ SILENT THINK TIME

26. Qi (pronounced "Chi") is the activity within body tissues and their ability to adapt to changing circumstances. It represents the interface where mind and body meet and is influenced by emotions and diet.

    Qi functions throughout the body, through specific pathways called meridians and chakra channels. Blood flow or climatic factors such as cold, wind, heat or dampness correspond to bacterial or viral illnesses. In Japan, shiatsu, meaning "finger pressure," is often used by large firms to reduce stress and cause relaxation, which results from a balanced flow of Qi.

27. People, in general, do not feel connected to each other. Therefore, having relationships is difficult, but it is so important to melt away the loneliness. It is so important to give love, so we can receive love. We must not get love confused with giving materialistic things or escaping to the unknown; these attitudes avoid what we truly need—love. Unconditional love increases our longevity through higher harmonic vibrational energies, as experienced through the Eastern practice of Deeksha, or the Christian "laying on of hands" hand energies.

    When I was 19, my roommates were a former nun and a former monk (they eventually got married). With their guidance, I performed a "laying on of the hands" on a classmate who had cerebral palsy, and watched her walk for the first time in her life. She then remained on crutches, out of the wheelchair. I was fortunate to be part of that miracle. She lost weight and regained the density in her very thin legs. The point is that energies can be controlled to flow and can heal others.

28. Dr. Hartmut Miller from Germany developed a new paradigm of physics called global scaling. His original formula states that the distance between planets, stars, whole galaxies; between electrons and nucleons; the optimum ph of human blood; and everything else in the material universe follows the same

mathematical structure. Matter is the results of an energetic continuum of vortexes of energy taking on increasing density.

STT and the Brain

29. For the best benefits of meditation, the frontal lobe of the brain needs more activation of dopamine, the essential neurotransmitter. Lack of dopamine increases a person's urge to maintain self-will and resist merging with the greater reality. The solution can only come about with an actual change on the physiological level which liberates the individual will from its struggle against surrendering to a greater reality.

    People with attention deficit disorder, addictions, aggressive behaviors or those constantly playing computer games have low dopamine imbalances.

    Willpower can be strengthened like a muscle through psychic calisthenics.

    "Our brains operate on three levels: I will, I won't, and I want," says psychologist Kelly McGonigal, author of *The Willpower Instinct* and professor at Stanford University. "For many of us, the I-want part wins." Addictions to drugs, alcohol, hoarding or behaviors like gambling are wrecking many lives.

    "Willpower can be trainable and cultivated," according to Roy Baumeister, a psychologist at Florida State University who wrote a book called *Willpower*. He states that the brain evolved from the back to the front; the back is the wanting part and the front is the restraining part. Through use of STT and meditation on the pineal and pituitary gland areas, we can turn off the switch of I-wants.

30. Dr. Eugene Peniston of the V.A. Medical Center in Fort Lyon, Colorado, and Dr. Paul Kulkosky at the University of Southern Colorado, conducted sophisticated biofeedback research on this topic. According to their studies, chronic alcoholics and

children of alcoholics often have less alpha brainwave activity than non-alcoholic individuals. This finding suggests that a deficiency of alpha and theta brainwaves predisposes an individual to the development of alcoholism or other substance abuse.

Even more dramatic was their finding that alcohol enables many of these substance abusers to achieve alpha wave activity, even though it was at an unacceptable cost to health, their bodies, relationships and success in life. This finding coincides with the suggestion that addicts are searching for an experience of attunement, oneness, or inner harmony and peace albeit in a dysfunctional manner. Furthermore, many unhealthy, compulsive behaviors such as alcohol abuse, smoking, overeating, caffeine consumption, and sexual addictions are actually the result of our inability to handle stress in our lives. (ref #30)

Thus the emerging field of addictionology seems to share a common denominator with the insights of philosophy, religion, and biophysics.

31. Much of our music is intended to stimulate rather than to relax. Its physiological effect is to dominate and override the natural rhythm of the heart by "entraining" it to the rhythm of the beat. In physics entraining is the process whereby two objects, vibrating at different speeds when they are separated, start to vibrate at the same speed when they are brought close to each other or connected by some form of energy exchange.

Dr. Hans Selye and Dr. Norman Cousins from the Sixth International Montreux Congress on Stress lecture; states music affects the electromagnetic field characteristics of the membrane of a cell. We now know that every cell in our bodies is affected by the sounds of music. We resonate physically; and our blood pressure, basal metabolism and brain beta waves denote stress from music. By bringing appropriate music and sounds into our life, we can keep our physical and psychological being in tune. You can actually assist your cells and organs to relax and renew themselves.

At Baltimore's St. Agnes Hospital, carefully selected classical music was provided in the intensive-care units. "Half an hour of music produced the same effect as ten milligrams of valium", says Raymond M.D. head of the coronary-care unit. "Patients who had been awake for four straight days were able to go into a deep sleep." (ref #30)

There is a different benefit to these more complex types of music, according to psychologist Frances Rauscher, Ph.D, and neuroscientist Gordon Shaw, Ph.D, of the University of California at Irvine. They say that complex music enhances our spatial intelligence—the ability to "see" the world accurately. They have shown that the spatial IQ scores of college students go up after hearing ten minutes of a Mozart sonata and that musically inclined preschoolers' puzzle building skills improve as well. Every style of music has its own purpose and viability. Our job is to learn how to choose wisely what will increase our own health and happiness.

32. We need to be "living in time" in order to experience present moment awareness and allow all suppressed inner imbalanced feelings to surface. For instance, when we submerge our bodies in a bathtub of warm water, without pausing between breaths, we are only aware of our immediate surroundings. It is our willingness to become aware of our imbalances that restores balance to the quality of our experience. Being addicted to constant gratification, we leapfrog past the present moment into plotting our next acquisition, always running ahead of ourselves, ignoring the flow of life. Our unconscious addiction to the mental habit of "living in time" is an attempt to escape the discomfort within our emotional body (ref. 29).

◄ SILENT THINK TIME

Are you trying to run away from fear or negative past memories, guilt or hate? The mind is unable to deal with these powerful emotions so it creates another problem – the addiction. Normally people don't want to get out of their addictions because that behavior keeps them from feeling their negative past fears. The brain then turns this emotional problem into a neuron track, thus making the problem biological, not just psychological. By the time realization sets in, the problem has often become very extensive, because the body has taken over, now creating a more difficult external problem. This is why it is so important to develop awareness and willpower, before the body gets physically ill, trying to make you alert to the seriousness of the addiction.

Being in the presence of now requires abundant oxytocin (the love, open-heartedness and gratitude hormone); sufficient dopamine (an important mid-brain neurotransmitter needed to feel vibrant, focused, with good concentration); and low levels of cortisol (the stress hormone that keeps our feelings balanced and our ability to embrace ourselves for who we are).

33. Conflicts – interpersonal or group disagreements that arise from differences in opinion, judgment, and values could be resolved by problem solving, wherein the aspirations of both parties are met. Usually this approach requires mature participation, frank communication, creative thinking, and the ability to compromise as needed. Through respect and getting beyond our own self-pity, dismissiveness, sarcasm, and sense of injury can we truly manifest respect for others. Do not forego lasting relationships in a quest for vindication, self-righteousness, or an unsatisfied ego. Always listen and empathize but ask yourself "Do you want to be 'right', or do you want to be happy?"

Reflective listening involves repeating to the other person in your own words what he or she said. Listening is being attentive; and fully present at the moment, not looking at your mobile

UNIVERSAL ACKNOWLEDGMENTS

device or impatiently waiting for a chance to interrupt so you can start talking again. Listening is not just a period of silence in a conversation for you to plan your next move in launching a counterattack. Listening is like the rain: it is nourishing and soothing, which leads to meaningful pauses, clarifications, and a connection and understanding in all our relationships. (ref# 31)

Lessons Philosophy

Daily physical exercise is needed to rid the body of toxins and to tighten muscles to keep the spine erect, thus keeping our minds alert. While standing, do a tense rolling motion of your entire body, beginning with the feet, legs, then the abdomen, buttocks, chest, arms, neck, and to the top of the head. Follow it with total relaxation afterwards. It is great for moving energies through our muscles, lymphatic meridian system, and our chakra auric energy vortexes. With that exercise our energy auras are then easier to feel.

After doing physical exercises, focused, slow, deep breathing helps recenter and calm our bodies, in preparation to quietly do the self-introspection STT lessons. It is always very important to show gratitude throughout your STT exercises.

Doing the daily exercises, breathing techniques and STT lessons will stimulate our willpower; enhance the ability to focus and concentrate; reestablish our intuitive self; and keep us motivated toward the correct positive pathways in life. Early morning is the preferred time to assimilate this information; otherwise perform the STT lessons at break times or any stressful times.

Early each morning, we need to set aside a minimum of 15 minutes, preferably 50 minutes, for self-introspection. Children of all ages and adults should recheck their behaviors throughout the day, preferably in the morning and before bedtime if possible. Adults can use their mid-morning and mid-afternoon breaks to accomplish this self-introspection.

We need to have the STT rooms installed at home, such as a screened-off area in the bedroom. We need to ask our bosses for the opportunity to improve productivity. School principals need to use their allotted quiet times to curb students' negative behaviors. Hospitals and nursing homes could use a designated room to calm themselves during stressful situations. Because airports produce so much noise, sound, air pollution and chaos, rattling our cells, travelers can certainly benefit and chill while waiting several hours before their flights.

Due to the constant, unchecked, all-absorbing stimuli of our five senses, we do not intentionally focus on perfecting our positive qualities; thus, we fail at developing ourselves as human beings. The solution is to follow this daily regimen of focusing and concentrating to improve ourselves. If performed in school, home, work or institutional environments daily at specific times, STT would be accepted as a ritual to reevaluate ourselves and our behavior and would curb many societal problems now and in the future.

We need the still, quiet, inward focus of introspection in order to function better throughout the day and to learn from our strengths and weaknesses. Worrying thoughts are like a poisonous drug to our minds. It is important to avoid letting even one single worry thought enter our minds. We must change our daily activities to encourage only positive thinking.

We have relationships for the wrong reasons: material greed, physical or aesthetic attraction, social position, idealism and vocational similarity. We would make better choices if we centered ourselves

◄ SILENT THINK TIME

with mental unity by doing the STT lessons and learning the magnetic qualities of wisdom, understanding, consideration and all-around efficiency.

Review and share your thoughts from the next chapter, "Letting Go," before beginning the STT lessons.

Letting Go: Freedom From Beliefs and Ego Release

In today's world we are trapped in the illusion that we must be in constant competition with one another. We live in the belief that you and I are different and separate; we're ignorant and devoid of the interconnectivity among all living energy elements in our world.

This chapter is offered to make you aware that we are all parts of the same cosmic harmony. When we realize that our essence is identical to the essence that makes up the cosmos, we overcome fear, sadness, envy and anger (ref. 21).

Here are some thoughts to help you become aware of this harmony, and to free you from old beliefs and release your ego so that you can achieve harmony with the world.

1. Do you listen merely with your ears or with your entire body? When sitting very still, with all your attention not fixed on anything in particular, your mind is very quiet and attentive, you can hear everything, sounds that are close and those far away. You can also "hear" the silence.

   Your mind is not keeping any sounds from entering; it is not condemning or judging; it is completely open, all-inclusive, without walls or barriers around it.

SILENT THINK TIME

2. Do we truly share with others, or are we thinking only of our own desires, attachments, emotions and thoughts? Every situation is an opportunity to share. When we are consumed with our own thoughts, ideas, opinions and emotions, we simply cannot see all the numerous opportunities to share. When we project our own ideas onto people, we draw conclusions about others and don't give them the space or freedom to change or be seen for who they are. If they do change, we do not see it. We only see our projection, not the person.

3. The word *discipline* actually means to discover, watch, observe and learn who we are. When we learn that, we can then learn about everyone else, because everybody basically operates the same. So when you know yourself, you know everybody else.

4. When we are constantly trying to grasp onto books or teachers for their "authority" rather than taking responsibility for our own authorization, we want to blame someone else for our own lives. At every moment we're creating our own future. It is easy to find fault with others but really there is no one to blame but ourselves. When we see who is really responsible, our attitude shifts from blaming others to appreciating every moment as the true teaching.

5. The more we get in touch with our own vulnerability and morality, the more we appreciate life and the preciousness of each moment. Life is the real teacher. The beginning of accomplishment is realizing the preciousness of life.

6. Do you identify with the street bums, junkies or winos, or is it easier to blame them for their problems, to despise others, to feel pity or to keep your distance? Or do you own your shadow side by not disowning aspects of yourself, therefore treating everyone equally?

7. How can we really know what we have unless we have experienced losing it? While we have it we don't appreciate it. Only after we lose it do we really value what we had.

LETTING GO: FREEDOM FROM BELIEFS AND EGO RELEASE

8. Usually we're fighting the flow, trying to swim upstream, wanting something we cannot have, having something we don't want, and always struggling. It's this kind of desiring and seeking that keep us from being free.

   Stop fighting, follow the flow of the stream, go with it and it's no longer painful. It's like two hands that are constantly struggling against each other. As soon as one hand stops resisting, the other hand also can go free. Our relationships are the same way. All a person has to do is give up trying to be right; step aside, be selfless and let go.

9. We're always searching for permanence, wanting good wonderful things to last forever and painful moments to end quickly. We fear change, so we create beliefs that reinforce the illusion of security and safety. We are afraid we will lose what we have attained – families, jobs, homes, positions, possessions, knowledge and accomplishments. Our fear of change and our greed for control have caused us to become attached to what we have and how we live. We have slowly been stopping the flow of the river from bringing fresh new water to revitalize our stagnant pool. Little by little we have been deadening our experience of life and our intuitive selves.

10. Our mind cannot accept the fact that life, like a river, is forever moving, flowing and changing. It fears impermanence and insecurity. So it builds walls around itself to protect its very existence, the walls of ME and MINE, MY beliefs and ideas. These walls limit our experience of life's reality. They give us the illusion of protection, yet they cause us to live in confusion, fear, and misery, isolated and struggling to maintain their little world. Life is flowing endlessly, constantly changing and attempting to break down these artificial walls we have made.

11. We identify with our bodies being separate from the sun, mountains, rivers, trees, flowers, grasses and other elements of the natural world. This belief is what keeps us self-conscious, watching, judging, and bound and imprisoned in our beliefs. We create an "inner me" rather than an "outer me," separating ourselves

from the world around us and eluding harmony. It is very important to understand that how we react to events affects all those around us, and how we are interconnected.

12. When there is fear, you know you are once again creating a barrier between yourself and the world, between yourself and others.

13. As scientists, artists, teachers, therapists or whatever occupations we hold, we get locked into a fixed position, an egotistic view of what reality is. Our downfall comes when we can't relate to others, disharmony occurs, and we guard our self-centeredness, rather than letting the river of life flow and accepting the differences. We become blind to everything but our own view. We can't see it's just one view so why get tied up with it? Every perspective is just a piece of the pie, not the whole thing.

14. How strong our addiction is to wanting to be right, even when it costs us nothing less than our freedom, happiness and peace. Due to our ego trip we choose instead to be fragmented, disenchanted, and suffering with loneliness, fear, anxiety and depression, rather than to admit we were wrong.

15. We have regrets about the past and fear the future, although these are just concepts and projections with no content in the present moment. If fear stands in the way, then maybe it's time to shatter the glass house in order to reconstruct it, this time without being picky and choosy.

16. To "let go" of the concepts of who we are, it takes courage and trust, a willingness to face fears and doubts, a realization that most of our thoughts are just preconceived ideas. The more willingly open you are to "let go," the more faith you have.

17. A quiet spacious mind looks like death to the little mind. By sitting in a stable way, like a solid rock, we become more centered, not fixed on our ideas or opinions, but more flexible, fluid, yet strong -- like a tree that can bend when hit by wind and rain.

LETTING GO: FREEDOM FROM BELIEFS AND EGO RELEASE

18. The more undeveloped the intuition is, the more distorted the ego image will be by this false identity, delusions and chaotic existence of error. Therefore ask in SILENT THINK TIME to direct your intuition so that you should know what to do about your problems.

19. Your thoughts, mind, body and self are only concepts. Thoughts are a measurement comparing the past, present and future. Thought consists of memories of the past which is already gone. You cannot control it so you try to control the future, which is unpredictable, so you suffer from trying to maintain this impossible control.

20. The "fight or flight" response is our mind's creation. It is constantly engaged in always becoming. Ask yourself "Who am I?" or "What is the ultimate truth?" or "Where did I come from?" There are no answers to these questions; it's just tricks played by the mind. When our questions disappear, we disappear. Just keep asking questions. The observer then becomes the observed.

21. We all are "escape artists" in managing success. We come alive when we do things; otherwise, we are dead. If we are just living because we are afraid to die, then we are all escaping death. If we get to our core existence, we can start living happily. To reach this happiness, find an STT area and find your core.

22. Perceptions change when we change the feelings attached to our thoughts. Reprogram your feelings and your thoughts will change. Everything is converted to a conviction or a habit, due to past experiences in consciousness, making the same negative movie shown repeatedly on your subconscious movie screen. You must resolve your past issues, silence the demons of the past and work toward "anger-less anger." Love is the best solution to all problems.

23. After any conflict in your world, repeat these words hundreds of times if necessary and with deep sincerity: "I will forgive, forget and let go!"

◄ **SILENT THINK TIME**

24. People are not afraid of the unknown; they are afraid of losing the known. When you see everything as a game, with opposites always played out on our conscious screen of drama, and you accept it, life is so simple then. You must accept "what is," then love can exist. Life is a mystery never to be solved, so stop trying to control the past, future and present.

The following are sayings from Sri Amma Bhagavan based on the Oneness Blessing (Deeksha). They show the difference between holding onto ego and old beliefs, and letting them go in order to achieve harmony.

SAYINGS FROM THE ONENESS BLESSING

The Awakened One	The Un-Awakened One
Does not seek greatness	Does seek greatness
Responds to circumstances	Creates circumstances
Lives in humility	Cultivates humility
Has nothing to oppose	Has something to oppose
Is not afraid of the truth	Is afraid of the truth
Allows destiny to be created	Tries to create destiny
Experiences freedom from one's own ideas	Is caught up in one's own ideas
Witnesses things happening	Tries to make things happen
Knows the world governs itself	Thinks the world must be governed
Does not try to impose one's will	Tries to impose one's will
Never expects results	Always expects results
Looks inside oneself	Looks outside oneself
Cannot cling to good or bad	Has to cling to good and bad
Is balanced	Is not balanced
Has no problem with wealth for wealth isn't the problem	Has a problem with wealth for the sense of possession is the problem
Sees everything as perfect	Sees everything as imperfect
Acts without possessing, interfering, or expecting anything	Acts with possession, interference, and expectation

LETTING GO: FREEDOM FROM BELIEFS AND EGO RELEASE

Is what one is	Is what one is not
Knows no attachment	Knows nothing but attachment
Knows no fear	Knows nothing but fear
Experiences nothing but consciousness	Tries to understand consciousness
Owns things but are not owned by them	Owns things & ends up owned by them
Has no cause for his joy, thus nothing affects his joy	Only knows pleasure, pain, and joy and depends on all happening
Experiences all the time	Dreams all the time
Lives in the mystery of what life is	Tries to understand what life is
Has allowed things to happen their own way	Tries to make things happen their own way
Has nothing to defend, thus does nothing to feel secure	Has to defend, thus must do things to feel secure
Does not try to control the future	Tries to control the future
Connected to everything	Is not connected to anything
Arises from the heart	Arises from the head

K-12 Students' Early Morning Lessons and Exercises

It is important that this lesson is done in complete silence, ignoring all distractions. Try to do it early each morning.

Review and discuss the chapter "Letting Go: Freedom From Beliefs and Ego Release." Use handouts or put the lesson on the board, listing the chapters each exercise refers to.

Please again remind everyone of the importance of no talking or other distractions during this lesson.

Sometimes one creates a dynamic impression by saying something; sometimes one creates a significant impression by remaining silent. The quieter you can become, the more you can hear.

Following are the chapters and appendixes that are to be used in this section:

(1) Letting Go: Freedom From Beliefs & Ego Release
(2) K-12 Students' Focus on What If? & Why?
(3) Did You or Will You Do This Today?
(4) Appendix A: Some Suggested Sayings to Spark Ideas
(5) Appendix B: Some Favorite Poems and Affirmations for Ideas

K-12 STUDENTS' EARLY MORNING LESSONS AND EXERCISES

(6) Appendix C: Positive, Affirmative Words For A Happier Life
(7) Appendix D: Negative Downfall Words That Destroy A Happy Life

1. **Step 1 is to silently think how you will answer the questions, always stating how you are grateful for the people, things or events pertaining to the following questions:**

    a. Pick out a question from "K-12 Students' Focus on What If & Why" from (2) above.

    b. Pick out a question from "Did You or Will You Do This Today?" from (3) above.

    c. Pick out a saying from "Appendix A: Some Suggested Sayings to Spark Ideas," from (4) above.

    d. Pick out a poem from "Appendix B: Some Favorite Poems and Affirmations for Ideas," from (5) above, or another favorite "feeling" poem.

    e. Pick out words from the lists in "Appendix C: Positive, Affirmative Words" and "Appendix D: Negative Downfall Words That Destroy a Happy Life," from (6) and (7) above, or list your own words. Explain that both positive and negative words are to be used in a positive manner in the writings.

    f. Make a notation of how many positive words vs. negative words are used in your vocabulary daily. Think about the allocated positive and negative words on the board and how you will respond to the negative words in a positive manner, still using the negative word in the sentence you will create. For example, Derek is a bossy bully. Today Derek says he is not going to be a bossy bully. Instead he is going to be courteous, compassionate and understanding.

2. **Step 2 is to do an energization exercise.**

    a. Jogging in place for 1 minute, imagine you are sucking in air molecules and energy from across the room, from your

SILENT THINK TIME

bedroom, from across the city and all the way from your favorite camping lake.

b. Twisting at the waist, swing your arms till your hands hit your buttocks for half a minute. Imagine you are throwing all your negative words used today or in the past outward from the tips of your fingers.

c. Reach your fingers to your toes, followed by stretching your arms to each side with fingertips outward, followed by stretching your fingertips far above your head. Repeat for 1 minute. Imagine you can touch the clouds, touch your favorite person in another place, and touch the cool lava in the middle of the earth.

d. While standing, use a tense rolling motion of your entire body muscles, beginning from your feet, lower legs left to right, upper legs left to right, hips, buttocks, stomach, left torso, right torso, left arm, right arm, left neck, right neck. Follow with complete relaxation. Repeat 4 times. While doing this exercise imagine your spine is a Christmas light string and your energy from exercising can light up each bulb as you are moving up and down your body with the tension and relaxation.

e. Do jumping jacks for 1 minute, while opening the palm of your hand. Imagine you are physically throwing any negative thoughts from the tips of your fingers, so the bad people, events or things are gone forever.

3. Step 3 is to put your head down on the desk or table for a minimum of 1 to 15 minutes or as long as possible, while trying to close out or dim your five senses.

a. Your arms should droop toward the floor, with arms and legs feeling like they weigh 1,000 pounds.

b. Focus and concentrate on what answers you will give to the questions on the board or handouts.

K-12 STUDENTS' EARLY MORNING LESSONS AND EXERCISES

   c. If a problem is bothering you, ask yourself, "What can I do about it in a positive manner?" While thinking of the problem, imagine attaching it to a cloud and watch it float away; or imagine putting it in a basket and watch it float down the river and out to the ocean.

   d. If you have a negative habit or pain that is difficult to get right of, focus and concentrate on its location in your body. Imagine a switch at that location. Now just turn off that switch, just as you would a light bulb switch. While focusing on it, will it to be gone forever.

4. **While staying silent, sit perfectly upright as if a string was pulling the top of your head. Then do the following self-introspection exercise on the board or handouts, to the best of your ability.**

   a. Look at the "Did You or Will You Do This Today?" list.

   b. Write sentences, sayings, or your own philosophical self-improvement poem, story or drawing.

   c. Describe what "good cypercitizenship" is.

   d. Or write an email or letter to your imaginary or dead influential relative who would love to hear how well you have been progressing. What would you say in it? What color of paper would you write it on? How would you make it smell?

5. **It is very important you share the lesson results with the class, counselor, family or a friend. While sharing what you have written, ask yourself why you responded the way you did.**

6. **Review your lesson results in the next week and month to see how your attitudes may have changed.**

K-12 Students' Focus on "What If?" and "Why?"

This corresponds with the prior lesson called "K-12 Students' Early Morning Lessons and Exercises."

Suggested What-If Questions for Grade School Students

1. If you were an ice cream, what kind would you be?
2. If you got a million dollars, what would you do first? Would you give any of it away or save it?
3. If you could go on a paid vacation, where would you go? Why?
4. If you could be a superhero, which one would you be?
5. If you could buy a new car or toy, which one would you buy?
6. If you took a pill that could make you live forever, what would you try to accomplish first?
7. If you could transform into an animal or bug because aliens were taking over earth, which animal would you be?
8. If you could go into the future or the past or both for an hour, what would you like to accomplish?

K-12 STUDENTS' FOCUS ON "WHAT IF?" AND "WHY?"

9. If you could get rid of all your material possessions except for one, what would you keep?

10. If you knew you would live 100 years longer, what would you try to accomplish?

11. If all your worries, fears and angers could be dissolved by a pill, would you take it if no side effects were to be experienced?

12. If you could imagine a "what-if" question what would it be?

13. If you were going to be blind in one month what would you want to see before it happens? What if you could not feel your touch? Taste? Hear? Smell? How would you react?

14. If you had an extra amount of time, would you take a nap, read a book or call a friend?

15. If you turned into a bubble and could float over any countries, which ones would it be?

16. If you went on vacation, whom would you take with you: your mother, father, brother, or sister?

17. What do you want your next Halloween costume to be?

18. If a disaster were to strike the earth, what animal would you want to turn into?

19. If your pet goldfish, dog, cat or turtle could talk, what do you think it would say?

20. If you could be on your favorite TV show, which one would that be?

21. If you took a pill and grew 100 times bigger than anyone else and had 1,000 times more strength, how would you help humanity? Would you rebuild roads? How much would you eat daily?

22. What if you took a pill and shrank to be 5 inches tall? What would you be afraid of? What could you do that other humans could not do?

◀ **SILENT THINK TIME**

Suggested What-If and Why Questions for Teens, Adults, Counselors, Businesses, Institutions and Organizations

This corresponds with the lesson called "K-12 Students' Early Morning Lessons and Exercises."

1. Review the "Suggested What-If Questions for Grade School Students" in this chapter.

2. At your next meal, focus and concentrate on the taste sense. Was it sweet, hot, sour, plain, fibrous, salty? What color? Texture? Shape? Can you imagine yourself in a restaurant you own, making this dish and selling it to others? What else do you want in your restaurant?

3. Focus and concentrate on smell. What do you smell first? Is it sweet, pungent, fruity, flowery, spicy, foul? Write or draw or act out what it smells like. How would you incorporate it into a career? Stop fires? Make a famous perfume? Invent a new chemical for technology? How would this apply to a career? Enhance your cooking?

4. You woke up being the world's most famous artist. Who would that be? What would you create first?

5. If you were to fly to the moon on an expedition to find the world's most needed mined minerals, how would you prepare yourself?

6. If you woke up being in charge of millions of restless people, what policies and goals would you establish first? How would you coordinate, organize and apply your concepts?

7. If you were a rescuer after a large disastrous earthquake, how would you be sympathetic to the needs of everyone around? What would you do first? Would you play the role of a teacher, clergy member, doctor, nurse, social worker or salesperson?

8. If you could make a recommendation to your teacher, counselor, boss, etc., of a way to improve our society, what would it be? How would you suggest approaching this problem?

K-12 STUDENTS' FOCUS ON "WHAT IF?" AND "WHY?"

9. If you are an extroverted, sensitive, judgmental, rational person, how do you think your most frustrating situation now could be improved?

10. If you are an introverted, intuitive, perceptive, feeling person, how do you think your most frustrating situation now could be improved?

11. What is most important to you now: family happiness, economic security, freedom, adventure, achievement, recognition or health?

12. Which category do you best fit into: realistic, investigative, conventional, enterprising or social? How does knowing that change your life?

13. Hundreds of millions of computers in the world go obsolete yearly, as do refrigerators, air conditioners, washing machines, dryers, etc. These contain plastics, aluminum, iron, tin, copper, nickel, zinc, gold, arsenic, silver, cadmium, mercury, rhodium, platinum, titanium, cobalt, plus 20 other minerals that are getting into our dumps on earth. If you were in charge of your neighborhood dump, would you require some of these to be recycled or defused to prevent damage?

14. Is your interest in repairing? Serving? Negotiating? Correlating? Assembling? Planning? Autonomy? Variety? Social contacts? Security? Appraising?

15. What 25 characteristics from the lists in Appendix C and Appendix D would you want in your marriage or best friend relationships? Your family relationships? Your neighbor relationships? Your teachers/counselors?

Did You or Will You Do This Today?

This corresponds to the prior "K-12 Students' Early Morning Lessons and Exercises" chapter. Did you do this today with the attitudes and feelings at the top of each list?

Compassion

1. Hug yourself
2. Do a favor for somebody
3. Thank someone sincerely
4. Spend money or time for another person rather than for an item for yourself
5. Be receptive, open and courteous to all around you, even if others were not
6. Be optimistic
7. Try nonsexual intimacy
8. Have self-confidence
9. Feel caring and belonging
10. Have an open mind
11. Do an act of charity

DID YOU OR WILL YOU DO THIS TODAY?

12. Respectfully share and help with others' troubles
13. Be considerate by being sympathetic to the struggles of people in different areas of the world
14. Be responsible, thoughtful, forgiving
15. Do what was expected of you: i.e., wash dishes/floors/clothes; clean your room; cook a meal; go shopping for someone; wave to the neighbor; smile to your boss -- all without selfish motives
16. Love the world as much as yourself

Self-Discovery

1. Be aware of your strengths and weaknesses
2. Spend money or time for another person rather than for an item for yourself
3. Be receptive, open, and courteous to all around you, even if others were not
4. Be optimistic
5. Be self-aware 100 percent of the day
6. Be self-introspective and reason out any disadvantages of anger
7. Reason out the benefits of positive kindness
8. Be totally content inside your own skin
9. Have a secure mind
10. Recognize fears and bad habits and talk yourself out of them
11. Lay a responsible basis for your future with your actions
12. Be aware of your shortcomings or weaknesses and overcome them with your strengths
13. Ignore dramatically self-absorbing actions or try to curb these behaviors

14. Rid yourself of your bad habits: anger, grouchiness, stubbornness, selfishness, envy, greed, picking your nose, alcohol, drugs

15. Realize and rebalance your life after knowing your dog or cat was being treated better than your family, friends or associates

16. Walk away from gossip or envious insults that were reinforcing others' egos

17. Avoid being an "emotional firefly" and spend more time on emotional connections

18. Display balance

19. Learn values… compassion… understanding…

Attachment

1. Try not to have attachments to material items, people, situations, bad habits

2. Ask yourself what are anger and attachment

Success

1. Write a journal entry about your future dreams and how to achieve them

2. Show success by being determined, courageous and self-confident

Ego-Control

1. Control your strong will or ego so as not to hurt anyone

2. Be humble and modest without pride

3. Let your ego feel itself in others through practical sympathy

4. Understand when our reality illusions and ego are dissipated

Positive Mindset

1. Ignore negative comments or behaviors or try to stop them
2. Approach today with enthusiasm
3. Speak only of someone's good qualities
4. Praise others for their positive efforts
5. Prop up somebody with an inferiority complex
6. Fulfill your positive goal and your positive attitude

Peace

1. Reflect harmony in any way
2. Stay silent to give a better dynamic impression rather than speaking out

Step back two steps, and view yourself as an outsider would see you. Then ask yourself or do the following:

1. Watch your thoughts. Don't run from pain or try to stop it, just experience it and it will disappear. Teach yourself to become aware of the emotional negative "messenger" that flows behind the scenes of our physical world experience, sent by our omnipresent power. Be ready to become your own ghost buster to exorcise the ghosts of the past in the dream called "time." Ask, "What specific emotional reaction did this event or person trigger within me?"
2. "When before this incident did I experience the exact same emotional reaction?"
3. "What does this remind me of?"
4. "Who used to behave like this toward me?"
5. Take a deep breath to move out of the triggering situation to keep yourself cool and conscious.

◂ **SILENT THINK TIME**

6. Say the following affirmation: "I restore my inner balance with my full loving attention without fear and judgment."

7. Invite pain and discomfort as friends to assist you and not hurt you, while taking slow deep breaths.

8. Compassionately feel the physical, mental and emotional sensations that you have so long been taught to suppress and run from.

9. Connect with your child-self with unconditional love, forgiveness and self-nurturing, without guilt, helplessness or neediness.

10. Reach back through time and space to rescue your child-self by bringing it into the safety of the present moment where you can give the unconditional love and attention it has been calling for. Otherwise, as adults we can never experience authentic peace.

11. Release your child-self with commitment, consistency and sincerity in order to release the adult emotional charge that is the source of all distractions and imbalances.

12. At about age 7, we begin preparing to enter the adult world, willingly walking away from our childhood. Have you made peace with your child-self by releasing all the conflicting childhood debris?

13. Crying is the release of the negative emotional charge that causes so much imbalance in our adult experience. Therefore, when we cry it is not for the adult, but it is for the stagnant blocked energy of the numb, neglected and emotionally abandoned child-self. Have you reawakened the child-like joy and creative parts in your shared inner adult-child subconscious?

14. Consciously neutralize the vibrational parental, peer group, or negative interactions with your broader physical world experience. Avoid, resist and deny any negative emotional charge.

15. Emotional balance requires achieving a state of acceptance within ourselves in which we no longer have an agenda about

DID YOU OR WILL YOU DO THIS TODAY?

what emotions we desire to experience. The opposite negative emotional charges are reduced by doing dramatic acts to gain attention and acceptance from others or sedation (i.e., alcohol or drugs) and control (a dysfunction of our male side to gain power over the discomfort). Are you emotionally balanced or do you vent negativity by being a drama queen or king or a control freak?

16. Are you a reactive person (adding fuel to the fire) who gets upset, blames, and then feels guilt, regret and shame? Or are you a responsive person (throwing water on the fire) who examines the notion of "becoming upset," and knows blaming is a means to get sympathy so it takes the attention off the blamer and places it on someone else? Remember: To "blame" = to "b-lame."

17. Do you disempower your own soul by declaring it to be enslaved by feelings of guilt, regret or shame, or do you gracefully sidestep the urge to react and courageously, powerfully use self-control to break a lifelong knee-jerking dramatic habit?

18. Do you associate color, sound, taste, smell, touch, emotions or movement in your mental clarity when thinking of negatively emotionally charged people or situations?

Adults' Silent Think Time Thoughts

1. The quantum mechanical human body uses neuropeptides to form thoughts. These small molecules are used by nerve cells to communicate with each other, and they influence particular brain functions, like analgesia, reward, food intake, learning and memory. The process is like a transformation of atoms and non-matter into matter. A thought of fear is a neuron-chemical change, except we do not call it thinking. The landscape is not made of solid objects, but is clustering of hydrogen atoms for air and carbon atoms in trees and so forth.

    Therefore, every solid object, including our bodies, is proportionately as void as the intergalactic space. By understanding the quantum, we enter into a vaster reality, spanning from quarks to galaxies. At the same time, the behavior of quantum reality turns out to be very intimate to us; the faintest shadow-line separates the human body from the cosmic body (ref. 18).

    The body is made up of a hierarchy of systems, organs, tissues and cells. DNA is made up of organic submolecules, atoms and subatomic particles.

    Gravity holds our molecules in place. Light, radio waves, lasers and other electromagnetic forces travel through empty space; matter and antimatter seem to exist in coordinated universes that have no physical contact. Subatomic particles have spins that are matched to one another, and it doesn't matter how far apart in time and space the particles are – their spins can be matched at opposite ends of the universe.

What this implies is that the commonsense idea of local reality is true only at a certain level (ref. 18). Therefore, we should be able to change our thoughts to avoid negative behaviors and bad habits.

"Thought" has a primary purpose which is to understand practical matters, but it has become a dominant process. When it steps out of place, it can become humanity's enemy and create psychological miseries. Thoughts are electrochemical exchanges between the brain cells.

Thought is based on past experiences. Memory is gathered, which is knowledge. Movement of thought based on the past prevents a clear perception of the present. The present, the now, is living. Perception of the present through the eyes of the past, the residue of the past, is distorted. The thought of future is usually a projection of the past. So thought is movement in time – into past and future. Being based on experience, thought is limited because experience is limited.

2. Beliefs, Eternal Gratitude and Connectors. Extremely large elephants that are tied with small chains as they were as babies are still conditioned to believe they cannot break away, so they don't. They believe the rope can still hold them, so they never break free. How many of us go through life like these elephants, believing that we cannot do something simply because we failed at it once? Failure is a part of learning; we should never give up the struggle in life.

Some people signify their harmonious connection with the field of intention, and have made themselves available for success. It's impossible to get these people, called "Connectors," to be pessimistic about achieving what they desire in their lives. Everything that shows up in their life seems simple because they "think from the end," experiencing what they wish to intend before it shows up in material form. They are eternally in a state of gratitude, appreciation, humility, high energy, generosity, kindness, and loving, creative inquisitiveness about life. They avoid loud, opinionated, dominating people who wallow in the horrors of life.

As Dr. Wayne Dyer explains, Connectors will tell you that the imbalances in the earth such as earthquakes, volcanic eruptions and extreme weather patterns are the result of a collective imbalance in human consciousness. They'll remind you that our bodies are made up of the same materials as the earth, that 98 percent of our blood was once ocean water, and that the minerals in our bones were components of the finite supply of minerals on earth. They view themselves as one with the planet and feel a responsibility to stay in balanced harmony, in order to help stabilize and harmonize the universal forces, which get out of balance when we live in excessive ego. Connectors will tell you that all thoughts, feelings and emotions are vibrations, and that the frequency of these vibrations can create disturbances—not only in us, but in everything that is made up of the same materials (ref. 25).

A few of Dyer's steps for optimizing your capacity to be healed are:
- "You can't heal anyone until you allow yourself to be healed."
- "By raising your energy to a vibrational match with the field of intention, you're strengthening your immune system and increasing the production of well-being enzymes in the brain."
- "Don't ask to be healed. Ask to be restored to that perfection from which you emanated."
- "Seek out and cherish the silence."

Use STT to create your own reality.

3. Socrates said, "To know oneself is to know one's body and soul." To know the rhythm of the body, the melody of the mind, and the harmony of the soul, is what create the vibrating symphony

ADULTS' SILENT THINK TIME THOUGHTS

of life. To integrate and explore your energy body is to find the place where breath and emotions reside. Your mental body is where thoughts and obsessions can be mastered. Your intellectual body is where intelligence and wisdom can be found. And your divine body is where the Universal soul can be glimpsed (ref. 19).

4. All persons, regardless of their belief systems, can enrich themselves by realizing the Truth through Kriya yoga, while using some Kundalini yoga spinal exercises (ref. 6-7). Kriya yoga is a positive, scientific path for realization of Truth, free from the burden of philosophical ratiocination, fanaticism or sectarian ceremony. It is an eternal, direct method of communing with our inner infinite Self, our divine spirit (ref. 8). Practicing Kriya yoga initiates a sequence of physical and mental changes that affect the body, mind and soul simultaneously.

   Lahiri Mahasaya, the polestar of Kriya, believed in Incarnations of the Lord, to uplift the justice of righteousness. The inner Light and Illumination is the real Incarnation of the Lord which the yogi calls Oneness Union in the Yoga (ref. 8).

5. Another way of connecting to your inner self is through the Oneness Blessing (Deeksha). It is a simple loving, intentional, thought-patterned touch on the head that transfers the highest spiritual energies, given by initiated Deeksha givers. The giver holds the receiver in his or her awareness for a few minutes and allows Deeksha to flow. It awakens our connection with the oneness in everything and brings a growth in consciousness. Deeksha can be given at a distance of thousands of miles or to a large group of people all at the same time.

   It was established for healing the body of repetitive emotional patterns, resulting in greater comfort with oneself and facilitating a neurobiological shift. In relationships it enables a greater sensitivity and connectedness with the other, freeing one from

◂ **SILENT THINK TIME**

the limitations of judgments and conditioning. Success and prosperity begin with consciousness – a capacity to expand one's horizons of thinking and an understanding of the universe.

Deeksha does the following:
- Awakens creative potentials, abilities and intelligence
- Increases ability to learn
- Resolves inner conflict leading to inner peace and harmony
- Brings love to relationships
- Heals emotional hurts and reduces thought burden
- Evokes affection, friendship and a sense of connectedness with the other
- Awakens compassion
- Infuses vitality
- Heals the body by healing the mind
- Relaxes the body and relieves stress
- Helps build love and appreciation for the body
- Invokes auspicious energies
- Removes blocks that hinder success
- Makes a possible mental frame for abundance
- Initiates a journey into experiencing unconditional love and joy
- Initiates a journey into awakening and self-god realization (ref. 24)

In a Deeksha brain study, several persons had EEG brain maps recorded before and after they received Deeksha. Immediately after Deeksha, the prefrontal area of the brain was activated in the recipient. Alpha and theta activity increased by 60 percent, which reflects increased blood flow to the brain. The people were giggling and laughing, which activated the prefrontal area for joy, happiness and compassion.

6. Another technique for getting to your inner consciousness is to ground yourself. Visualize a cord of energy running from the base of your spine (root chakra), to the center of the earth. Through this

energy cord, release all extraneous negative thoughts. Whatever you're worried or upset about can safely be forgotten now (ref. 11). You can even imagine touching a friend with a positive thought with the cord touching them.

7. Auras extend up to 7 feet from the body, and have been called the eighth chakra. As you inhale or exhale deeply, stretch your arms outward to expand your space around your body.

The colors and shapes of your aura and chakras can be detected via aura-reading machines, which pick up the acupuncture meridians of the body's vibrational rates off the body organs. These machines are very accurate in defining personality characteristics and are used by government organizations and prisons. People who are healers have green auras; those who do a lot of logical thinking appear yellow; spiritual or meditating people frequently have violet highlights (ref. 11).

8. Chakras are energy centers which are part of the energy of the body. The energy, (Chi/Qi) acts as a bridge that connects the body to the soul. We have three body systems that sustain life: physical body (the perimeter around your skin), which we can feel and touch. The energy body is a soft sheath of energy encapsulating your body with three dantians (energy centers), which are the second, fourth and sixth chakras (ref. 21). Energies emit from the center of our palms and the center of the upper third of the sole of each foot. This energy body acts as a bridge connecting our physical and spiritual bodies.

Finally, the third life-sustaining system is a spiritual body that surrounds both the physical and energy bodies. These three bodies influence our physical, mental and emotional health.

9. The essence of the healing chakra is the use of energy to effect the completion of the soul. Without knowing energy you cannot know your soul. An imbalance in the energy body originates from thoughts, state of mind and negative energies. Your energy body

◀ SILENT THINK TIME

will be influenced accordingly, causing disease, illness or energy imbalance (ref. 24).

Chakras are awakened and activated through energy and can heal illness. Energy exists in three forms: light, sound and vibration. Vibration is the quickest way to approach stimulating the chakras on up through the brain stem. This is why we need to do exercises that activate all meridians; or dancing, hiking, playing drums or chanting.

By utilizing a natural healing power within all of us, people with a healthy, balanced vibration can heal themselves when confronted with illness. Just think vibrating Qi energy to flow to the area needing to be healed and it will be healed.

10. The seven chakras of the body are directly related to different areas of the brain. Qi energy is equivalent to electricity, and the chakras are the switches that turn on the various areas of the brain. In order for a human being to become one with the divine spirituality within, the whole brain must be awakened. This can be done by the exercises in the following chapter.

   Chakras have a direct symbiotic relationship with the autonomic nervous system, which controls our basic life functions for our respiration, circulation and digestion, and the endocrine system. Our primitive consciousness gets trapped in the lower three chakra levels, thus causing us to be obsessed with sex, money, addictions, and other physical and material desires. It is very important to awaken the chakras to higher levels, thus stimulating our wisdom, love, mercy and insight (ref. 21). Item 22 in the "Universal Acknowledgments" chapter explains the chakras in detail.

11. Chakra means "wheel of spinning energy" in Sanskrit. These seven personal vortices of energy aligned along our spines are the primary energetic link between subtle energy fields and our physical bodies, working together to form the auric field that surrounds us.

ADULTS' SILENT THINK TIME THOUGHTS ➤

The aura can expand or contract depending on feelings of security and comfort. Just because you cannot see it does not mean it doesn't exist. You can feel it if you focus on it. Unfortunately, when we are feeling threatened from our environment, we keep our aura stifled and pulled inward toward our bodies.

An auric field forms seven egg-like ovoids around our body, based on the seven chakra eye centers on our forehead and beginning between our eyebrows with the root chakra on the bottom of the column, stacking upward to the seventh chakra. Any energy field that touches or penetrates our auric field can give us an impression of thoughts, feelings and intentions that they contain. This auric membrane's size and color reflect your overall mental and physical health and emotional frame of mind.

12. Have you ever colored items in a coloring book in the shades you felt they should be, instead of what others agreed they should be? Have you felt tension where people have been arguing? Have you felt "good vibes" from a friend or person of interest? Have you felt uncomfortable or threatened when someone was moving too close to you? When somebody is "in our face" for whatever reason, your auric field causes you to feel threatened, thus making you step backward or pull your aura inward (ref. 11).

This vibrating energy of ours is based on our chakra energy vortexes and is referred to as our Qi/Chi. In an exercise in Qi Gong (ref. 10), you hold your hands in front of your dantian (low navel area). If you briskly rub your palms together for 1 or 2 minutes, then move them less than an inch apart, like you were squeezing a sponge between your palms, you'll feel a gentle pushing resistance. That is the boundary of the root aura.

Another example of how energies are felt in our human body is when we get near vortexes near the ground. When that happens, we feel our body lifting off the ground, even though we still are physically located in the same place.

◀ SILENT THINK TIME

Another example is when four small people can simply lift a very large heavy person up toward the ceiling with extreme ease. Begin by having the four people stand at the corners of the big person's chair. Next have each person put a right hand in front of themselves, as if they were stacking their hands in a pile, without touching each other's hands, with about three-quarters of an inch space between the hands. Then, in the same order, have each person place their left above the last person's left hand. Feel the energy flowing.

Now that each person has gathered energy from the hand pile, the two people near the big person's knees will clasp their own hands, with index fingers straight and thumbs crossed; they will place them under the sitting person's knees. Simultaneously, the two persons at the chair's back corners will place their hands in the same manner, except they will put them in each of the sitting person's armpits. At the same time, all four persons can lift that person's head to the ceiling with very little effort. That is chi energy flowing.

13. Your luminous body egg or aura is the energetic boundary around you that defines your personal space. Have you noticed how good it feels to lie on the ground by a lake or mountain, watching the birds or stars go by, or just being in the beautiful world of Mother Nature? These naturally ecologically balanced places are full of energy that helps to equalize our own energy systems.

    When we are hemmed in by the materialistic manmade world, we feel our need to escape to the forests, mountains, lakes or oceans to get our aura energies rebalanced. If you cannot do this then the next best place is the escape to the introspective STT room at home, work, a hospital, school or other place.

    We must recenter and rebalance our energies several times during the day to be functioning as whole positive, successful persons!

Adults, Businesses, Institutions & Organizations Healing Exercises

All adults can use STT to improve the clarity of their thoughts and improve future successes by doing these exercises, including the relaxation. Qi energy acts as a bridge connecting body and soul; therefore you must relax in order to meet with your soul.

Ask your spouse at home, boss at work, school principal, hospital administrator, assisted living or nursing home director, or prison chief, to create a STT room, where you can go for 15 minutes or more twice daily to balance and recenter your body so you can be more productive and peaceful the rest of the day.

See "Setting Up an STT Room" for guidelines. It's best to use the STT room before eating, or wait one or two hours after eating.

You should do some of the exercises from each numbered section in this chapter every day. Do the other exercises on alternate days.

Ego and Negative Thought Release Exercises

1. Begin by reviewing the "Letting Go: Freedom From Beliefs & Ego Release" chapter. Afterwards keep your eyes closed, with eyes

SILENT THINK TIME

upward toward the area between your eyebrows, during the introspective parts of this exercise.

2. Proceed by asking yourself how many negative vs. positive words you used in your vocabulary today and yesterday. Make the negative words into positive words, using similar sentences that you used when saying the negative words.

3. Pick a visualization exercise from the following list to help rid your mind of any negative thoughts, behaviors or bad habits. Everything that was created in this world was imagined first, so fearlessly place your imagination on what you want. You'll see it when you believe it! Assume the feeling of the wish you want fulfilled!

   - Imagine a cleansing tornado swirling around your body and removing any doubts, fears, narrow-mindedness, insecurities and grudges. As it swirls around you, it leaves clear, good, white light energy, and collects all the extraneous dark energy as it leaves.
   - Imagine a vacuum cleaner plugged into the center of the earth, sucking out any dark worries or resentments from your body's auric field, while your brightly shining chakras are aligned with this auric cord ascending upward through all your chakras.
   - Imagine a big broom coming by and sweeping any pain or illness away. Meanwhile, keep focusing on the body part you want healed.
   - Ask a brilliant white angel or divine spirit to spread its arms or wings around you to repair any damaged etheric energy web holes around your body that were caused by drugs or alcohol.
   - Visualize attaching all your bad habits, anger or hurts to the next cloud passing by. Or put them in a basket and watch them float down the river and out to the ocean.
   - Imagine sending positive, warm, loving thoughts over your own very long mental telephone wire to your favorite person. Ask them if they received it. When doing this be very aware of all colors, motions, smells and sounds.

- If the negative thoughts still do not go away, very forcibly throw your arms outward in the air to release all negative thoughts and energies.

4. The following exercises will help you remove negativity, making your actual quiet breathing and introspective time more effective.
    - If a very annoying person upsets you, step backward two steps to re-evaluate the situation. Imagine how water flows off a duck's back, and then proceed to ignore the upset. If you cannot ignore it, then try to avoid being in that position. If you want to help change the other person's negative behavior, then try to reason using only positive words.
    - If you feel you are under psychic attack from a negative person, maintain a strong auric cord of love to everyone who has ever loved you; and be as free as possible from guilt, doubt or fear. Immediately strengthen your luminous aura's shell to ricochet off any poisonous darts thrown your way; ground your energy body; and thank all your guardian angels or divine spirits, who are standing at arm's length from you, for helping push the negative energy away. Imagine the smiling faces of the people who love you, while feeling your positive image connecting with them. Be ruthless at tossing any intruders out.
    - The universe is unpredictable so you must go with the flow and have faith in its outcome. Keep expecting the uncertain and accept that you do not know the future. "Thought" is just a measurement comparing the past, present and future. Thought of the past (memories) is already gone and you cannot control it, so you try to control the future which is unpredictable, so you suffer.

Introspective Thoughts

1. Practice saying five to ten grateful, positive words of appreciation for all the wonderful people, things or events in your world today.

◄ SILENT THINK TIME

Ask yourself, "What was my most precious moment over the last day?"

2. Ask yourself or your divine image to lead you from restlessness to peace, from desires to contentment, and ignorance to wisdom. Be cleansed of all bad habits, keeping only noble thoughts while appreciating the beauty all around you (ref. 9).

3. Take notice of your true self: all strengths and weaknesses, inferiority complexes built into your armored, onion-layered shell. Ask, "What is my purpose? Why was I born?" "Who am I?" Practice integrity at all times.

4. Let your ego begin to feel itself through compassion and unconditional love for others. Ask yourself, "Is my soul my True Self?" and "If my body died, will my soul transcend into time and space?"

5. Imagine an evolution time line chart of our bodies made of earth, wind, fire, water and air. Imagine when you were conceived by your parents and the sperm and ovum met. Think of the feelings of life, love and creation felt just before that moment in time. Imagine the DNA's journey to the womb and the Mother Nature's light bulb igniting the cell division and multiplication of cells. Imagine the intellect, ego, instinct mind, forms, skin, eyes, taste, smell, speech, grasp, kicking feet, and the palpitation of the heart being all established by the 4th month. This heart beat is when time is established; therefore, our consciousness is established!

The time of conception of a human is the only time in our bodies when we use all 5 works of the Universe in our bodies: emanation, projection, preservation, withdrawal, and retention, per Amma Adi Sakthi.

6. Imagine vibrations going around a triangle with speeds of high, medium, and low, with a vortex in the middle. Next imagine a tabled matrix chart with all of our saints, gurus and sages in it; for example, Jesus Christ, Mother Teresa, Bhagavan Krishna, Osho, Matavatar Babaji, Paramahansa Yogananda, Lahiri Mahasaya, Sri Yukteswar,

etc. Finally, imagine those vibrating energies flowing from this matrix to and from the vibrating vortex triangle to and from earth. Ask yourself, which vibrations have you felt from the matrix?

Imagine You Are Gathering Chi/Qi Energies

Imagine you are gathering energy (ref. 10) while doing the following movements in each direction, as quickly as possible to awaken and energize your chakras with Kundalini yoga (ref. 7) or Hatha yoga exercises. Energize yourself by raising your vibrations of energy up with loving, grateful feelings, so you attract positive people, situations and things, rather than negative energies. While you're doing all these exercises, imagine a golden white ball of magnetic energy swirling around your body.

1. While standing and twisting at your waist, swing your arms so they reach behind your back. Let your arms stretch far behind, while imagining that you're grabbing armfuls of air molecules from your room, the neighborhood, and the entire city, and pulling them to your second chakra (below your navel).

2. While sitting with palms facing upward and arms outward, rotate your arms from small to large circles in each direction. Then imagine you're flying and pump your arms up and down as fast as you can.

3. While sitting, carefully rotate your neck in each direction and forward and backward while focusing on lengthening each vertebra. Then while bending at your waist, drop your head down in a circular grinding motion, breathing out any tightness.** Do this in both directions.

4. While standing, with palms together over your head and arms stretched as far up as possible, move arms outward from your sides, as you bend forward doing a swan dive. When palms are near the floor, do the reverse swan dive, still trying to gather Chi/Qi.

◄ **SILENT THINK TIME**

5. While standing, begin tensing and relaxing each body part from the left to the right sides, beginning with the feet, calves, thighs, stomach, buttocks, chest, shoulders, arms and neck, while imagining you are pulling Chi/Qi through each chakra point. Completely exhale to relax. Inhale. Reverse the process beginning at the neck and moving downward.

6. Standing on your toes, with arms at your sides and fingers extended, stretch your arms outward from your sides, forward and upward. Increase speed to energize the chakras.

7. Run in place for 1 minute, with heels lifted toward buttocks. Imagine you are pumping Qi from your heels all the way above your crown chakra.

8. Do the Kundalini yoga Breath of Fire (ref. 7). With arms stretched outward and thumbs pointed backwards, while sitting on a stool or floor, pant hard while pulling stomach in. Do for 1 minute.

9. Move your arms together in figure 8 patterns around your body to gain energies from each hemisphere of the brain. Donna Eden describes this as the Celtic Wave (ref. 12). This exercise improves flexibility, strength and the cardiovascular system while it stimulates the vital meridian energy flows.

10. Hold arms in front of you, squat, and then stand up, with arms still in front of you. Repeat for a minute. Increase your speed. Bless yourself with each movement.

11. Self-vibrate your chakras. Stand with your feet hip-width apart, arms loose and relaxed at your sides. Smile. Slightly flex your knees, while repeatedly springing up and down lightly on your toes. Feel the vibration move upward through each chakra. Your tongue should slightly touch the upper roof of your mouth. Move your waist forward, back and sideways, expanding the vibrations. Any stagnant energy in your chest will flow out through your palms and fingertips.

ADULTS, BUSINESSES, INSTITUTIONS & ORGANIZATIONS HEALING EXERCISES

Breathing Exercises

1. Do the following breathing exercises while focusing on breathing into your lower (stomach area), middle (chest rises up) and your upper chest (shoulders rise up). Breath, Prana yoga, is the single unifying bond that ties all humanity together. All share its instrumentality for sustaining life. Only breath, being universal, can lead to realization of the Truths, that is One pure consciousness of the ultimate self.

2. Do the Bhastrika power breath. With arms above your head, quickly pull them down in a snapping motion, as you exhale. Do a set of 10, then 15, then 20. Imagine with each exhale you are releasing any negative thought or habit. Be aware of the back of your throat's hissing sound, called the Uiju, when you exhale.

3. Balance and open up all your chakras by inhaling deeply into your lower stomach area, to the count of 1 and forcefully exhaling quickly to the count of 2, increasing the rhythm while focusing on the root chakra. Keep your eyes closed and turned upward. Note prior chakra information in the "Adults' Silent Think Time Thoughts" chapter. Continue this procedure for 1 minute for each of the seven chakras as you move upward through the chakras to the crown chakra.

4. While breathing deeply into your lower, then middle, then upper stomach, purse (circular in form) your lips and force the air out as fast and loud as you can. This expels all bad toxins from your body quickly. Do for 1 minute. Quit if you feel dizzy.

5. Breathe deeply into your lower, middle, then upper stomach, while placing your thumb over your one nostril. Exhale fast and loud through the open nostril. Repeat with the other nostril using your ring finger to plug the other nostril. Do for 1 minute. Quit if you feel dizzy.

6. Calm the breath while your arms are extended in front of you as long as you can. Inhale slowly while counting to 10. Hold for 10.

◂ SILENT THINK TIME

Exhale slowly for 10. After resting your palms upward near the tops of your thighs, repeat again for another minute while doing this for the count of 15, then 20. As you breathe deeply, you will not be oxygen-deprived. This technique slows down your heart activity, thus giving you longevity and relaxation.

Always do this with palms on thighs, and use throughout the STT, meditation or prayer. It also works great when you're stressed while caught in traffic, or your boss asks you a puzzling question, or your child pushes your "anger button."

7. Do the Bee Buzz, a modified "Om" sound, for a couple of minutes. Calm your thoughts by putting your thumbs lightly on your ears, index and middle fingers placed on your forehead and eyebrows, third fingers lightly resting on the very outer edge of your eyes, and little fingers on your cheekbones. While doing deep inhalations and deep Uiju exhalations, make a slight humming sound while you exhale. Listen closely to the sounds, feel the vibrations, and focus on the breaths.

8. While sitting in a comfortable position, relax with your palms turned upward near your thighs. Close your eyes and inhale into the lower, middle and upper chest. With your tongue on the roof of your mouth, elongate equally the sounds of "Ah…" "Oh…" "Um…" in a low pitch until your teeth feel the vibration. Repeat loud and deep while doing this in a high pitch: "Ah…""Ah…" "Um…". Finish in a medium pitch: "Ah…" "Oh…" "Um…".

Quietly Watch Your Thoughts

1. Sit on a stool or on the floor in an STT room in a meditative posture, with your palms near your thighs, palms turned upward in a receptive mode, index finger touching the tip of the thumb. Silently focus and concentrate on your third eye area between your eyebrows.

2. Imagine moving Qi from your root chakra on upward, through

each and all of your bodily chakras equally. Do you feel blocked or open, comfortable or stuffy at any of them? If so, visualize moving the Qi ball of energy past the blockage until it is a positive experience.

This third eye area is where your first through seventh chakra eye centers are, allowing you to control the energies from your lower root chakra up to your crown chakra. Place the index finger touching the thumb as you focus on moving energy from the red root chakra, through the orange low navel chakra and the yellow solar plexus chakra. Second, place the index finger in the middle of the thumb for the green heart chakra and focus on the energy flowing through it and the dark blue throat chakra. Third, place your index finger at the base of the thumb and watch the energy flow through the third eye eyebrow center, continuing up through the crown to the eighth chakra, which is the first auric field relating to the root chakra. Last, put your index finger in the middle of your palm through the rest of your meditating.

We have seven auric luminous egg bodies around us which relate to the seven chakras of energy up our spine and our stacked seven chakra eye centers between our eyebrows on up the forehead. (There is a further explanation in the "Adults' Silent Think Time Thoughts" chapter.) Around the luminous egg bodies we have an etheric web of energies.

3. Focus on some of the questions from the chapter "Did You or Will You Do This Today?" Teenagers should look at the "K-12 Students' Early Morning Lessons" chapter and do their introspection first.

4. By looking toward your third eye with eyes closed and pressing lightly on your third eye chakra, try to remember your grade school teachers' names and what they looked like. What were all your pets' names? Your neighbors' names and faces when growing up? Did you do better during this exercise than you otherwise would have done?

◂ **SILENT THINK TIME**

5. Do the total relaxation exercises.
   - Lie down with your feet mat-width apart and flopped outward. Arch your back so your shoulders are flat on the floor.
   - Inhale deeply through all three lung levels: lower, middle, upper. Tense both feet while raising them 3 inches above the floor. Continue tensing your buttocks, stomach, both arms while making hands into fists and raising them 3 inches above the floor.
   - Stick your tongue out as if you were going to touch your chin, while making a loud "Ahhh" roaring sound. Exhale quickly and then relax your entire body.
   - Next inhale, followed by tensing all body parts as explained in "Imagine Gathering Energies," item 5, but making a sour face, as if you had bitten into a lemon, while raising your head off the floor. Exhale quickly and then relax your entire body.
6. Stay relaxed in this lying down position for 5 minutes if possible, while focusing on your third eye area and watching all your thoughts float by. If you're aware then the rest is automatic.

The Awakened one sees everything in eternity and follows the flow of events, whereas the Un-awakened one sees everything in the immediate and resists the flow of events.

Self-Vibrate Your Chakras, Create and Review

The "Om" sound is especially effective in directly stimulating the brain to maintain balance and harmony among all the internal organs. Lowering the active brainwaves dissolves emotional fluctuations, such as grief and fear, etc. (note the solfeggio frequencies in "Universal Acknowledgements," item 24). The sound of "Om" has traditionally been the sound of Oneness, unity of all (ref. 21).

1. While sitting in a comfortable position, relax with your hands in the prayer position near your heart. Close your eyes and inhale

ADULTS, BUSINESSES, INSTITUTIONS & ORGANIZATIONS HEALING EXERCISES

into the lower, middle, and upper chest. With your tongue on the roof of your mouth, elongate equally the sounds of "Ah…" "Oh…" "Um…" in a low pitch. Repeat while doing this in a high pitch: "Ah…" "Oh…" "Um…" Finish in a medium pitch: "Ah…" "Oh…" "Um…"

2. Imagine the vibration from your body radiating, pulsating rhythmically, upward and outward from each of your chakras. Imagine opening the number of lotus petals at each chakra associating with the number of breaths: beginning at the four-petal coccygeal root chakra, the six-petal sacral spleen chakra, the 10-petal lumbar solar plexus chakra, the 12-petal dorsal heart center, the 16-petal throat center, and the 1,000 petals at the head and 2 petals at the medulla (ref. 8).

Review the Other Chapters

1. While staying quiet and silent with no distractions, review Appendix A and Appendix B. create your own affirmations or sayings, or write your own poem.

2. Imagine repeating to yourself many times "Forget, Forgive, Let Go" to any bad habit, negative energy degradations, or past negative events or energies. Think only love to those who hurt you.

3. Review the chapter "Did You or Will You Do This Today?" and answer some of the questions, while also creating your own question/statements to be used in tomorrow's STT session.

Healthy Hand Hugs and Using True Hugs Liberally

Hugs are an expression of compassion, unconditional love and freedom from ego.

Healthy Hug Day is a holiday on January 21 with the goal of allowing people to show more emotion in public.

Studies have shown that physical contact is indeed necessary for healthy social, psychological and physical development. Hugs strengthen the immune system, decrease the risk of heart disease, lower the levels of the stress hormone cortisol and increase levels of the "love hormone" oxytocin and the "feel good" brain chemicals serotonin and dopamine.

Babies who are frequently touched and hugged grow faster and healthier than babies who are not touched and hugged. Doctors, various metaphysical and Eastern healers, and shamans use finger energy to pull black spots of negative energies out in order to correct health ailments, especially pertaining to the immune system.

Some people shy away from being touchy-feely in public, but humans have always been social creatures who thrive through human-to-human contact. Hugging may be the best tonic of all for what ails you.

HEALTHY HAND HUGS AND USING TRUE HUGS LIBERALLY

All electron matter generates electrical and electromagnetic energy fields at a precise frequency, and these fields affect everyone and everything. People with disease and negative emotional states have lower frequencies, for example, a frequency of 100-250, whereas people with higher vibration or harmonic resonance have the energy of unconditional love or the Divine energy; their frequencies are 350-400.

So hug often to help keep your body healthy through high-vibrating auric fields, meanwhile spreading that good energy to everyone around you.

Adults, regardless of gender, you must be free and liberal with long, tight, arm-embracing hugs – unless you are in our school system or in the business world. We are not allowed in public schools or work to give a strong sincere bear hug, but we could formally establish the next best thing: a 5-second hand-to-hand high-5 frozen moment to make the other person feel the same message, still not violating the other person's physical torso space.

How can you practice this hand-to-hand high-5, and on whom? Who will be the next person you give a strong sincere bear hug to? Will you first look lovingly into their eyes, before giving them the hug?

All that truly matters in the end is that you have loved.

What Were the Results of Your Lessons?

Can you have faith and trust in the good in yourself and others, by fulfilling your noble positive goals and aspirations, improving your life and humanity?

Did you will new pathways to be formed and throw old habits outward so that success is to be blazed?

Did you reshape your own self-willed destiny with introspection and positive thinking, and have you reevaluated your daily duties after these lessons?

Did you fix attention on your specific positive goal with confidence and determination, followed with action?

Did you persevere until all obstacles were overcome, and perform all lessons in an introspective, sincere manner?

Did you go with the flow, similar to the "river of life," or did you try to control your world while staying in the side pond, because of insecure fears or stubborn beliefs? Or did you try to be a salmon and swim the hard way upstream?

WHAT WERE THE RESULTS OF YOUR LESSONS?

Did you change the world around you by having an STT room established at or near your home, work, school, hospital, nursing home, prison, airport or institution near you?

Did you use the STT room daily and/or multiple times?

Did you change the number of negative words you use daily?

Did you feel each of your chakra energies and make them flow smoothly and evenly?

Did you see or feel the Qi or auric energies around you?

Did you give gratitude often today and hug yourself and others?

Did you release any egotistical unneeded beliefs?

Are you an Awakened or an Un-awakened person now?

What did you do today that was special?

What sayings or poems did you create?

What was your favorite "What-if?" and "Why?"

Appendix A: Some Suggested Sayings to Spark Ideas

Compassion

1. Caring for or spending time with a loved one may be the most precious gift anyone could hope to give.

2. Compassion, tolerance and altruism bring happiness and calmness. Perhaps thought is my concept of spirituality.

3. Compassion is not violent, harming or aggressive and shouldn't be confused with attachment and intimacy.

4. The main cause of depression is not a lack of material necessities but a deprivation of the affection of others.

5. Reconciliation is compassion, respect for others' rights and views, gentleness and affection, and is indispensable in our daily lives.

6. Respect is deserved by compassionate, intelligent, knowledgeable, altruistic and admirable persons.

7. Help me never to judge another until I have walked in their shoes for a week.

8. All that truly matters in the end is that you have loved.

APPENDIX A: SOME SUGGESTED SAYINGS TO SPARK IDEAS

Faith

1. Faith dispels doubt and hesitation, reduces pride, liberates suffering, and delivers peace and happiness.
2. When you have faith in something, it's not faith, it's belief! When you have faith in nothing, emptiness is our true nature. Having faith in nothing is trusting in your true nature.

Forgiveness

1. Only when we're able to recognize and forgive ignorant actions from the past can we strengthen ourselves and solve the problems of the present constructively.
2. Judge not, and you shall not be judged. Condemn not, and you shall not be condemned. Forgive and you shall be forgiven.
3. To counteract ignorance, concentrate on your interdependence, to purify your notion of reality.
4. One who cannot forgive others destroys the bridge over which they themselves must pass.

Happiness

1. The essence of all happy lives is one's emotions and attitude toward others. Once you have pure and sincere motivation, all the rest follows.
2. Happiness and satisfaction come from having few material desires, self-cherishing thoughts or life's attachments.
3. Three things that most inhibit happiness: judgment of others, negative thoughts and envy.
4. Altruism -- motivation void of power and wealth -- so that justice, equality and happiness prevail first requires a staunch moral fabric.

◄ SILENT THINK TIME

5. If you humbly know your true self and your inferiority complexes of brittle imitation of deluded egotistical soul armor, you can find true happiness.

6. Our desires cause suffering and delusional dissatisfaction, thus contaminating our joy and happiness that would result in fruits of wholesome actions.

7. No one is in charge of your happiness but you.

8. Do you always want to be right or do you want to be happy?

Peace

1. Sometimes one creates a dynamic impression by saying something; sometimes one creates a significant impression by remaining silent.

2. Peaceful and tranquil external surroundings can cause limited disturbances.

3. Wasting precious moments and avoiding self-introspection are like indulging in poison. This is wasting our life away.

4. Ultimate success is tranquility and warm-hearted feelings for others; these derive from developing love and compassion.

5. The quieter you become, the more you can hear.

Positive Thinking

1. By giving we shall receive.

2. If I reflect harmony in myself, I can spread it to others.

3. If I want a genuine smile, I must first produce it.

4. Do not make any pain or suffering worse by worrying; instead, think positive thoughts.

5. To be aware of a single shortcoming in oneself is more useful than knowing 1,000 in somebody else. Speak only of their good qualities.

APPENDIX A: SOME SUGGESTED SAYINGS TO SPARK IDEAS

6. Mental development in harmony with material development is very important.

7. If you have willpower you can do anything, because you are your own master.

8. If struck by a poisonous arrow, first pull out the arrow without taking time to ask who shot it. Similarly, where we encounter suffering it's important to respond with compassion rather than the politics of choosing those we should help.

9. Pursue to the end the positive goals of being truthful and honest. Make reasonable choices for yourself and others; otherwise, regret will happen.

10. By pointing a finger at others, displaying our lack of positive attitude, we admit to our own faults.

11. By saying something positive and kind or nothing at all, or by swallowing evil words unsaid, no one ever has to give apologies or try to explain in hope of forgiveness.

12. The kindest word in the entire world is the unkind word never said.

13. Keep your eyes on the sun and you will never see the shadow.

14. He who hunts for flowers finds flowers and he who hunts for weeds finds weeds.

15. Get rid of anything that isn't useful, beautiful or joyful.

16. Happiness is not the goal, it's the by product.

Self-Discovery

1. Laziness stops our progress, and creates procrastination, inferiority and negative actions of non-virtue.

2. Cultivate inner-disciplined patience and ignore modern man's constant drive for the best, fastest, cheapest, at all costs.

SILENT THINK TIME

3. The ultimate authority must always rest with the individual's own reason and critical analysis.

4. Listening, not babbling, cultivates joy, stable mind, wisdom and wealth, and removes ignorance.

7. Self-discipline gives birth only to happiness, as a perfume's refreshing aroma travels spontaneously in all directions.

8. Become actively engaged in assuming responsibility, knowing no one else can afford to assume someone else's will to solve their problems.

9. Doubt is the beginning, not the end, of wisdom.

10. Having good manners simply means putting up with others' bad manners.

11. You make your bed you got to lie in it.

Success

1. Determination, courage and self-confidence equal success. Yet remain humble and modest without pride.

2. Every day we are given stones. But what do we build? Is it a bridge or a wall?

3. Instead of waiting for someone to bring you flowers, why not plant your own garden?

4. Don't be afraid to go out on a limb. That is where the fruit is.

5. When fate shuts the door come in through the window.

6. Luck is what happens when preparation meets opportunity.

7. Success is the quality of your journey, not a destination.

8. Nothing ventured, nothing gained.

9. Luck is the byproduct of loving and working hard.

10. The squeaky wheel gets oiled, so be assertive.

APPENDIX A: SOME SUGGESTED SAYINGS TO SPARK IDEAS

11. If you don't toot your horn, nobody else will do it for you.
12. A chain is no better than its weakest link.
13. United we stand, united we fall.
14. Winning is not everything, but wanting to win is.
15. If you do not know where you are going you'll end up someplace else.

Anger

1. If subconsciously we are angered, unhappy, dissatisfied and hostile, then the true source is our reality, which is misconstrued with a lack of awareness.
2. Indulgence is blaming others or fate if something unpleasant happens rather than descending into ourselves to learn why.
3. Anger, hatred and strong emotions may gain temporary victory, but the true hero is the one who gains victory over anger and hatred.
4. Embarrassed by anger or negative words you cannot take back? Then the only solution is to apologize or bite your own tongue before trying to say anything negative again.
5. Anger, hatred, confrontation and hostile attitudes only serve to heat up the situation; whereas a true sense of respect gradually cools down what otherwise could have become explosive.
6. Delusion is the real cause of problems, trouble and conflict. It forces one to be attracted to one's self-side, with hatred and anger on the opposite side.
7. Those who quarrel with others, instead of quarreling with their own hearts, waste their lives.
8. The person who pursues revenge should dig two graves.

◄ SILENT THINK TIME

Attachment

1. Attachment is blinding and leads to imagining a halo of attractiveness to the object of desire.

2. The satisfaction of sexual desire only by the possession of the other, rather than true friendship first, brings unrewarding, unlasting relationships.

3. Sexual attachment involves all five senses at the same time and thus has a powerful potential for problems, destruction, disappointments and a false illusionary addiction to love.

4. I started with nothing, and I still got most of it.

Change

1. A blossoming tree becomes bare and stripped in autumn. Beauty changes to ugliness, youth to old age, fault to virtue. Things do not remain the same; nothing really exists exactly as we see it. Thus appearances and emptiness exist simultaneously, like what we are made of: negative and positive atoms.

2. Too old too soon, too young too, too late.

Ego

1. Egotism, pride, greed, anger and the other ugly outgrowths of self-centeredness are barriers to our development.

2. Don't cut others down at the knees just to make yourself taller.

3. Self-centeredness is wasting a great opportunity, thus turning a troublemaker out into the community. Being a self that is centered is knowing who you are.

4. Criticism never built a house, wrote a play, composed a song, painted a picture or improved a marriage.

5. Envy is a waste of time. You already have all you need.

APPENDIX A: SOME SUGGESTED SAYINGS TO SPARK IDEAS

6. What other people think of you is none of your business.
7. Don't bite off more than you can chew.
8. Don't go barking up the wrong tree.

Fear

1. Look fear in the face and it will quit bothering you.
2. We have nothing to fear but fear itself.
3. Frame every so-called disaster with these words, "In five years, will these matters?"

Guilt

1. Guilt is hopelessness, discouragement, and past-oriented. Genuine remorse is healthy, future-oriented, responsible and hopeful.

Appendix B: Some Favorite Poems and Affirmations for Ideas

Love Is Patient

Love is patient, love is kind.
It does not envy, it does not boast,
t is not proud. It is not rude,
It is not self-seeking,
It is not easily angered,
It keeps no record of wrongs.
Love does not delight in evil
but rejoices with the truth.
It always protects, always trusts,
Always hopes, always preserves.
Love never fails.
And now these three remain:
Faith, hope, and love.
But the greatest of these is love.
     I Corinthians 13.4-8, 13 NIV.

Thoughts on Forgiveness

He who cannot forgive others destroys
The bridge over which he himself must pass.
  George Herbert (1593-1633)

APPENDIX B: SOME FAVORITE POEMS AND AFFIRMATIONS FOR IDEAS

When a deep injury is done to us,
We never recover until we forgive.
   Alan Paton (1903-1988)

If There Is Light in the Soul

If there is light in the soul,
There will be beauty in the person.
If there is beauty in the person,
There will be harmony in the home.
If there is harmony in the home,
There will be order in the nation.
If there is order in the nation,
There will be peace in the world.
   Chinese proverb

Peace, Love Faith

Make me an instrument of peace;
Where there is hatred, let me sow love;
Where there is injury, pardon;
Where there is discord, union;
Where there is doubt, faith;
Where there is despair, hope;
Where there is sadness, joy;
Where there is darkness, light.

Grant that I may not so much seek to be consoled as to console,
Not so much to be understood as to understand,
Not so much to be loved as to love.
For it is in giving that we receive,
In pardoning that we are pardoned.
   Saint Francis of Assisi (1181-1226)

◄ **SILENT THINK TIME**

You Look for Life's Garden

Buried dead disappointments in the cemeteries of yesterday;
I plow the garden of life today with creativity;
Sowing seeds of wisdom, health, prosperity and joy;
Watered with good judgment, kindness and respect for all;
The perfume of peace flows like sun rays
Through all of life's garden, if you only look for it.
    Karen Z. Stryker

Gandhi's Seven Dangers to Human Virtue

Wealth without work,
Pleasure without conscience,
Knowledge without character,
Science without humanity,
Business without ethics,
Religion without sacrifice,
Politics without principle.

Success

When we think of failure
Failure will be ours.
If we remain undecided
Nothing will ever change.
All we need to do
Is will to achieve something mighty
Then simply do it.
Never think of failure
For what we think,
Will come true.

APPENDIX B: SOME FAVORITE POEMS AND AFFIRMATIONS FOR IDEAS

Whenever beauty is perceived, ugliness arises.
Whenever good is perceived, evil arises.
Existence gives rise to non-existence,
And confusion brings about simplicity.
High gives rise to low,
Noise brings about silence,
The truly wise man goes about doing nothing
While teaching without words.
He possesses all and achieves unity with everything.
He produces, but does not possess.
He rounds off his life but does not claim success.
Because he does not claim, he cannot lose.

Without Love Will Make You

Belief Without Love Will Make You fanatical,
Duty Without Love Will Make You ill-humored,
Order Without Love Will Make You narrow-minded,
Power Without Love Will Make You violent,
Justice Without Love Will Make You severe,
A Life Without Love Will Make You ill.

I asked for strength ...
And I got a challenge to make me strong.
I asked for wisdom ...
And I got problems to solve.
I asked for prosperity ...
And I got brain and brawn to work.
I asked for courage ...
And I got danger to overcome.
I asked for love ...
And I got troubled people to help.
I asked for favors ...
And I got opportunities.
I received nothing I wanted
I received everything I needed (ref. 23).

◂ SILENT THINK TIME

> True happiness
> ...is like the butterfly.
> The more you pursue it
> ...the more it will elude you.
> But if you are patient
> ... It will come to softly land on your shoulder.
>   Chinese proverb

Imagine a World......

GONE IS: the greed;
   the battle of the wills;
      judgmental anger;
         hate;
            resentment;
   Misunderstandings; blame; high expectations.....
IMAGINE A WORLD WITH: glowing happiness;
   Positive vibrations flowing between every being;
      Unconditional love;
         Selfless godly vows inside all;
            Stress-free and care-free
               And time is of no essence.
IMAGINE A CLEARING BETWEEN STORYBOOK HUGE TREES:
Brightly colored flowers and waterfalls flowing over many landscapes;
   Vibrating colors in the many rainbows in the sky;
      Gardens filled with abundant vegetables and fruits;
         Softened self-reliant hearts bubbling with miracles.
IMAGINE A CIRCLE OF PEOPLE OF DIFFERENT RELIGIONS
HOLDING HANDS
Christians worshiping and praying with unconditional love instilled by God's graces,
   While on pilgrimage between their richly decorated churches;
Hindus seeking pursuit of Truth, oneness to God, Son, & Holy Ghost through cosmic vibrations,

APPENDIX B: SOME FAVORITE POEMS AND AFFIRMATIONS FOR IDEAS

    To evoke joy, peace, wisdom, self-realization, humbleness & spirit enlightenment;
Buddhists praying to Buddha,
   Trying to be free from the inner spirit's endless cycle of birth and death;
American Indians with colorful feathers, dancing to a pow-wow beat,
   Connecting with the animal and land spiritual energies;
Islamics bowing to their black meteorite stone temple,
   Praying for peace;
Jews worshipping mysteriously while locked into history,
   Sharing a forever badge of blame;
Shintoists' myths honoring their past,
   Worshiping their originated rich intricate shrines in natural splendor;
Taoists teaching virtue, righteousness, subservience,
   If only all had a piece of their humility;
Tibetan Lamas' cultural treasury of historical tombs,
   Teaching the true strengths of our inner souls;
ALL SIMPLY FOCUSED ON A PEACEFUL PRESENT;
ALL BASIC NEEDS FULFILLED AND STRONG DESIRES WANING;
ALL REASSURED THEIR TRANSITION FROM LIFE TO DEATH ALREADY HAS ITS DESTINY;
ALL COMBINING THE STRENGTHS OF EACH RELIGION INTO ONE BELIEF;
ALL INCORPORATED INTO ONE AND ALL;
ALL HUMANITY HOLDING HANDS,
     SMILING, CONTENT, FOR THE SAKE OF PEACE
      WHAT A BETTER WORLD IT WILL BE.

by Karen Z. Stryker

SILENT THINK TIME

AFFIRMATIONS
by Karen Z. Stryker

Through my deepest expanded consciousness meditation or STT, I will consciously receive the white light from my divine angels, feeling its warmth as it passes through me. Seeing your consciousness is like a blind man seeing color.

I am the captain of the ship of my judgment, will and activity. I will guide my ship of life, through all the channels toward positive thinking, compassion and non-volatile ports.

May I open the gates of solitude and see myself standing in the colorful flowers, lush gardens, with an angel looking down on me, answering all my questions.

Oh divine spirit, teach me to till the soil of my mind's garden with discipline and sow it with the seeds of good habits.

Before getting out of bed in the morning, I will affirm to radiate my cheer to everyone I meet today. I will be the mental sunshine for all who cross my path, spreading magnetic warmth.

Oh divine spirit, teach me to discipline my senses, and to substitute for bodily temptations the greater temptation of a bright clear aura and soul happiness.

I will be the resistless, warm, glowing fire of energy of positive thinking. My divine joy smile will light their hearts to put a smile on their faces.

I will expand my little bubble of joy. I will keep puffing at it with the breath of concentration until it spreads all over my face, into my heart, throughout my entire body and mind and deep into my infinite consciousness.

APPENDIX B: SOME FAVORITE POEMS AND AFFIRMATIONS FOR IDEAS

Oh divine spirit, teach me to make my mind garden produce blossoms of beautiful positive thoughts, thus the flowering of beautiful peaceful memories.

May my desires lead me to do STT or meditation daily, diving deeper and deeper until I find the immortal pearls of answers to my questions, wisdom and joy.

Now that I have drowned out the jostling crowds of desires and wild cravings, I can feel the bliss and be the wise chief in control of the city of my brain's thoughts.

May I be surrounded only by serene, unconditional loving, understanding, sympathetic, selfless, honest, considerate, humble, appreciative friends. My reflection of these qualities will then draw these types of people to me.

I was born with a clear, bright, solid soul and aura. I vow never to allow bad habits to destroy it, sending me to withered hopes and fruitless aspirations. I will do my STT, expressing my gratification for everything around me, before allowing that to happen.

Appendix C: Positive, Affirmative Words for a Happier Life

Ponder how you relate to each of these words.

Pick one to five per day and start with each one to write about how to improve your world.

Note that there are more positive words than negative words in our dictionaries, but we use more negative words in our daily conversations.

ACCOMPLISHED	AMUSING	CANDID
ACHEIVEMENT	APOLOGETIC	CAREFREE
ADAPTIVE	ARTISTIC	COOPERATIVE
ADJUSTED	ASTUTE	CAPTIVATING
ADORABLE	ATTENTIVE	CHARISMA
ADVENTUROUS	AUSTERITY	CHARITABLE
AFFECTIONATE	BALANCED	CHARMING
AFFILIATED	BEAUTIFUL	CLEVER
AGREEABLE	BELIEVABLE	CHEERFUL
APPRECIATIVE	BELONGING	COMICAL
ATTRACTIVE	BEWITCHING	COMPLIABILITY
ALLURING	BEWITCHING	COMMON-SENSE
AMBITIOUS	BIGHEARTED	COMPASSION
ANGELIC	BRAINY	COMPOSED
ALTRUISTIC	BRILLIANT	CONCENTRATION
AMIABLE	CALMNESS	CONSIDERATE

APPENDIX C: POSITIVE, AFFIRMATIVE WORDS FOR A HAPPIER LIFE

COOPERATIVE	GOOD-LOOKING	KINDNESS
COURAGEOUS	GOOD-NATURED	LISTENER
COURTEOUS	GORGEOUS	LITERATE
CUNNING	GRANDEUR	LIVELINESS
CUTE	GRATEFUL	LOVING
DELICATE	GRATIFYING	LOYALTY
DELICIOUS	HANDSOME	MAGNETISM
DELIGHTFUL	HARD-WORKING	MAGNIFICENT
DEPENDABLE	HAPPINESS	MELLOW
DETERMINATION	HARMONIOUS	MODESTY
DILIGENT	HILARIOUS	MOTIVATED
DIGNIFIED	HONORABLE	NOBLE
DIPLOMATIC	HONEST	NONBELLIGERENT
DISCIPLINED	HOPEFULNESS	NEUTRALIST
DISCREET	HOSPITABLE	NONARROGANT
ELEGANT	HUMOROUS	NONATTACHMENT
EMPATHETIC	HUMANITARIAN	NONCONTROLLING
ENCHANTING	HUMBLE	NONEGOTISTICAL
ENJOYABLE	HUMILITY	NONGREEDY
ENLIGHTENING	IDEALISTIC	NONIGNORANT
ENTERPRISING	IMPRESSIVE	NONJEALOUS
ENTERTAINING	INCORRUPTIBLE	NONJUDGMENTAL
ENTHUSIASM	INDUSTRIOUS	NONMANIPULATIVE
FANTASTIC	INSPIRING	NURTURING
FAVORABLE	INTELLIGENCE	NONPERFECTIONIST
FASCINATING	INTERDEPENDENT	OBEDIENT
FAITH	IDEALISTIC	OBSERVANT
FOCUSED	IMPRESSIVE	OPEN-HEARTED
FORGIVING	INCORRUPTIBLE	OPEN-MINDEDNESS
FRIENDLY	INDUSTRIOUS	OPPORTUNIST
FUN	INSPIRING	OPTIMISTIC
GAY	INTELLIGENCE	ORDERLY
GENEROUS	INTERDEPENDENT	PASSIONATE
GENTLENESS	INTRIGUING	PATIENCE
GENUINE	INTROSPECTIVE	PEACEFULNESS
GIVING	INTUITIVE	PERSEVERANCE
GLAMOROUS	JOYFUL	PERSONALITY
GOOD-HEARTED	JUSTICE	PLEASANT

◀ SILENT THINK TIME

POLITE	PRINCELY	STABLE
POSITIVE ATTITUDE	PROMISING	STILLNESS
PRACTICAL	PROSPEROUS	STOIC
PRAGMATIC	QUIET-MANNERED	STYLE
PRAISEWORTHY	QUIET-WITTED	SUPERB
PRINCELY	RADIANT	SUCCESSFUL
PROMISING	RAVISHING	SWEET
PROSPEROUS	REALIZATIONS	SYMPATHETIC
QUIET-MANNERED	RECEPTIVE	TACTFUL
QUIET-WITTED	RECIPROCATING	TENDER-HEARTED
RADIANT	RECONCILIATING	THOUGHTFUL
RAVISHING	REGARDFUL	TOLERANT
REALIZATIONS	RELIABLE	TRANQUIL
RECEPTIVE	RESPECTFUL	TRUSTWORTHY
RECIPROCATING	RESPONSIBLE	TRUTHFUL
RECONCILIATING	REVERENCE	UNCONDITIONAL LOVE
REGARDFUL	RIGHTEOUSNESS	UNDERSTANDING
RELIABLE	ROMANTIC	UNGRUDGING
RESPECTFUL	SATISFIED	USEFUL
RESPONSIBLE	SAVORY	VIBRANT
REVERENCE	SECURE	VICARIOUS
RIGHTEOUSNESS	SEDUCTIVE	VIGILANT
ROMANTIC	SELF-CONFIDENT	VIRTUOUS
SATISFIED	SELF-CONTROLED	VIVACIOUS
SAVORY	SELF-DISCIPLINED	WARM-HEARTED
SECURE	SELF-ESTEEM	WELL-BALANCED
ORDERLY	SELFLESS-NATURED	WELL-EDUCATED
PASSIONATE	SELF-PRESERVATION	WELL-FAVORED
PATIENCE	SELF-REFLECTING	WELL-MANNERED
PEACEFULNESS	SELF-RESTRAINT	WELL-PROPORTIONED
PERSEVERANCE	SENSUAL	WISE
PERSONALITY	SENTIMENTAL	WELL-THOUGHT-OF
PLEASANT	SERENE	WILLFULL
POLITE	SHARING	WINNING
POSITIVE ATTITUDE	SINCERITY	WITTY
PRACTICAL	SKILLFUL	
PRAGMATIC	SMILING	
PRAISEWORTHY	SPIRITUAL	

Appendix D: Negative Downfall Words That Destroy a Happy Life

Reflect within your life and reevaluate how you have used these negative words.

Pick out one to five each day, and write down how to covert these into positive daily words.

While thinking of the word throw your arms upward and outward like you're physically throwing that word out from the palm of your hand. Rid your mind of these words.

ABNORMAL	ATTACKING	CALLOUS
ABSURD	AUTHORITARIAN	CARELESSNESS
ABUSIVE	BEASTLY	CLUMSY
AMBIGUOUS	BLAMEFUL	COLD-HEARTED
ANGER	BOORISH	CONCEITED
AGGRESSIVE	BOSSY	CONDESCENDING
ANNOYING	BOTHERSOME	CONFRONTATIONAL
ANGRY	BRUTAL	CONFUSED
ANXIOUS	BULLY	CORRUPTNESS
APATHETIC	BULL-HEADED	COVETOUSNESS
ARROGANT	BURDENSOME	CRITICAL
ATTACHMENT	CALUMNY	CROOKED

◂ SILENT THINK TIME

CRUDE	FUSSY	MEAN
DECEPTIVE	GREEDY	MEDDLER
DEMEANING	GROUCHY	MILITANT
DEMENTED	GRUFF	MISERABLE
DESIRES	GUILTY	MISREPRESENTED
DESPONDENCY	HATEFUL	MOODY
DISAGREEABLE	HAUGHTINESS	NAGGING
DISAPPROVING	HARSH	NASTY
DISCOURTEOUS	HESITATING	NAUGHTY
DISCOURAGED	HOARDING	NERVOUS
DISGRUNTLED	HOPELESS	NOISY
DISHONEST	HORRIBLE	NONTRUSTWORTHY
DISILLUSIONED	HOSTILE	NONVIRTUOUS
DISORDERLY	HOT-HEADEDNESS	OBNOXIOUS
DISORGANIZED	IGNORANT	OBSTINATE
DISREPUTABLE	ILL-HUMORED	OFFENSIVE
DISRESPECTFUL	ILL-MANNERED	OPINIONATED
DISTURBING	IMBECILIC	PATRONIZING
DIVISIVE	IMMORAL	PERFECTIONIST
DRAMATICAL	IMPROPER	PERTURBED
EGOTISTICAL	IMPATIENT	PESSIMISTIC
ENRAGED	IMPOSSIBLE	POMPOUS
ENVIOUS	INCOMPETENT	POUTING
EVASIVE	INDECENT	PREJUDICE
EXCESSIVE PRIDE	INDIFFERENT	PROFANE
EXPLOITABLE	INDIGNANT	PROVOKING
EXTRAVAGANT	INDULGING	QUICK-TEMPERED
FEEBLE	INFERIORITY	REACTIVE
FEROCIOUS	COMPLEX	RESENTFUL
FLAMBOYANT	INFLEXIBLE	RIGID
FIERY	INSECURE	ROTTEN
FILTHY	INTOLERANT	ROWDY
FOOLISH	IRRATIONAL	ROUGH
FOUL-MOUTHED	IRRITABLE	RUDE
FRANTIC	JEALOUS	SCOLDING
FRENZIED	LYING/LIAR	SELF-ABSORBED
FROWNING	LOUD	SELF-CENTERED
FURIOUS	LUSTFUL	SELF-CHERISHING

APPENDIX D: NEGATIVE DOWNFALL WORDS THAT DESTROY A HAPPY LIFE ➤

SELF-DESTRUCTIVE	SULKY	UNSETTLED
SELF-DECEPTIVE	TEMPERAMENTAL	UNWILLINGNESS
SELFISHNESS	TROUBLESOME	VIOLENT
SHALLOW	TYRANNICAL	VULGAR
SHAMEFUL	UGLY	VULNERABLE
SKEPTIC	UNBALANCED	WHINEY
SLANDEROUS	UNFAIR	WICKED
SLOPPY	UNGRATEFUL	WRETCHED
SHEEPISH/SHY	UNHAPPY	WORKAHOLIC
SOLEMN	UNJUSTIFIABLE	WORRISOME
STINGINESS	UNPLEASANT	WORTHLESSNESS
STUPID	UNREASONABLE	
STUBBORN	UNRELENTING	

◄ SILENT THINK TIME

Dear Reader:

If you have suggestions on how to improve our schools, businesses or society in general, through SILENT THINK TIME, please email me at silentthinktime@msn.com . I would welcome the opportunity of sharing your ideas with other readers in a future book. Thanks!

Karen Stryker

References

1. Min Ha (France), "Bees Detect Pollution"
2. The David Lynch Foundation, http://dlf.tv/2010/transcendental-meditation-in-arizona-schools/
3. Vivian Goldschmidt, M.A., "The Bone Health Revolution," www.saveourbones.com
4. Sherry Brescia, "Great Taste No Pain," www.GreatTasteNoPain.com
5. Genevieve Lewis Paulson & Stephan J. Paulson, "Chakras, Auras & the New Spirituality," Llewellyn Publications, 2010
6. Skakta Kaur Khaba, "Kundalini Yoga – Unlock Your Inner Potential Through Life Changing Exercise," Dorling Kindersley
7. Gurmukh, "Kundalini Yoga," Gaiam DVD
8. Swami Satyeswaranananda Giri, "Kriya – Finding the True Path," The Sanskrit Classics, 1991
9. Paramahansa Yogananda, "Metaphysical Meditations," Self-Realization Fellowship 1964, www.yogananda-srf.org, (323) 225-2471
10. Francisco Garripoli & Daisy Lee Garripoli, "Qigong," Gaiaim DVD

◄ **SILENT THINK TIME**

11. Cynthia Sue Larson, "Aura Advantage – How the Colors in Your Aura Can Attain Your Desires and Attract Success," LIghtworker Publications, 2006

12. Donna Eden, "Energy Healing With Donna Eden," Innersource, www. Innersource.net

13. Michelle Kluck, CMT, "Massage Practice Acupressure," Gaiam DVD

14. Michelle Kluck, CMT, "Reflexology," Gaiam DVD

15. Bodo J. Baginski & Shalila Sharmon, "Reiki Universal Life Energy – Heals Mind, Body, Spirit, A Holistic Method Suitable for Self-Treatment and Home Professional Practice Teleotherapeutics/ Spiritual Healing," Life Rhythm Publications, 1985

16. Osho, "Body Mind Balancing – Using Your Mind to Heal Your Body," St. Martin's Griffin

17. Dharma Singh Khalsa, M.D., and Cameron Stauth, "Meditation as Medicine – Activates the Power of Your Natural Healing Force," Pocket Books, 2001

18. Deepak Chopra, M.D., "Quantum Healing – Exploring the Frontiers of Mind/Body Medicine," Bantam Books, 1989

19. "What are Solfeggio Frequencies & HZ Meditation?," "The Six Original Solfeggio Frequencies," www.youtube.com/watch?v=tOmMr3FHTOw

20. "Say Omm," Time magazine, February 21, 2012

21. Iloni, Lee, "Healing Chakra – Light to Awaken My Soul," Best Life, 2005, 2008

22. Carola Beresford-Cooke, "Acupressure – A Practical Introduction to the Benefits of This Therapy," MacMillian Quarto, 1991, page 7

23. Gurmukh, "The Eight Human Talents – The Yoga Way to Restore the Balance & Serenity Within You," Harper Collins Publishers, 1997, page XXXIX, Introduction

REFERENCES

24. Amma Bhagvan, www.onenessuniversity.org

25. Dr. Wayne W. Dyer, "The Power of Intention – Learning to Co-create Your World Your Way," Hay House, 2004

26. http://www.holistic-mindbody-healing.com/harmonic-resonance.html

27. http://www.rexresearch.com/articles/roffe.htm

28. E.J. Clark & Alexander Agnew, Ph.D., "The Ark of Millions of Years, Volume Three 2012 – Unlocking the Secret," 2008, www.arkofmillionsofyears.com

29. Michael Brown, "The Presence Process – A Healing Journey into Present Awareness," 2005, Namaste Publishing

30. Self-Realization Magazine – Winter 2011 Vol. 83 No. 1, 3880 San Rafael Ave., Los Angeles, Calif. 90065-3219. www.yogananda-srf.org, (323) 225-2471. They referenced Susan Smith Jones, Ph.D, at UCLA, who wrote The Joy Factor:10 Sacred Practices of Radiant Health (Conari Press)

31. Self-Realization Magazine – Spring 2012 Vol. 83 No. 2 www.yogananda-srf.org, (323) 225-2471

32. Jnanavatar Swami Sri Yukteswar Giri "The Holy Science", Self-Realization Fellowship, 1894

33. Joseph Selbie & David Steinmetz "The Yugas – Keys to Understanding Our Hidden Past, Emerging Energy Age, & Enlightened Future", 2011

34. "A Paul Davids Film – Jesus In India", www.jesus-in-india-the-movie.com Sundance

About the Author

Karen Zalubowski Stryker earned five college degrees: two in education, psychology, computer science and art; and seven teaching endorsements; and taught grades K-12, most of the time in the high school.

Karen's additional careers were systems analyst, co-owner of RV, Tent and Cabin Resort, and co-owner of the first video store west of the Mississippi.

She is a writer, poet, painter, silversmith, home builder and creator of large tile murals. She hikes, does art shows, and has traveled in many countries She has lots of stories to tell of her backpacking, hosteling adventures and living with families in some of the 42 countries she has traveled to. She tries to do ½ hour of SILENT THINK TIME twice daily after doing 15 minutes of exercises.. Note the unfinished bottle building photos mentioned in "Set Up An STT Room" chapter.